*The Life Recovery Bible,
Genesis* contains actual
pages from *The Life
Recovery Bible,* providing
a concise introduction to
all of its features. Turn to
the User's Guide for a
review of these features
and for information
about their placement in
the Bible.

The Life Recovery Bible
will be available for
purchase after September
1, 1992 at your local
Christian bookstore. If
you cannot locate a store
that carries this Bible, call
Tyndale House Publishers
at 1-800-323-9400.

The Life Recovery Bible
will be available in
softcover, hardcover, and
deluxe bindings.

THE *Life*

Tyndale House
Publishers, Inc.
Wheaton, Illinois

GENESIS

BIBLE

The Living Bible

THE TWELVE STEPS

1. We admitted that we were powerless over our dependencies—that our life had become unmanageable.
2. We came to believe that a Power greater than ourselves could restore us to sanity.
3. We made a decision to turn our will and our life over to the care of God as we understood him.
4. We made a searching and fearless moral inventory of ourselves.
5. We admitted to God, to ourselves, and to another human being the exact nature of our wrongs.
6. We were entirely ready to have God remove all these defects of character.
7. We humbly asked him to remove our shortcomings.
8. We made a list of all persons we had harmed and became willing to make amends to them all.
9. We made direct amends to such people wherever possible, except when to do so would injure them or others.
10. We continued to take personal inventory and when we were wrong promptly admitted it.
11. We sought through prayer and meditation to improve our conscious contact with God, as we understood him, praying only for knowledge of his will for us and the power to carry it out.
12. Having had a spiritual awakening as the result of these steps, we tried to carry this message to others, and to practice these principles in all our affairs.

The Twelve Steps used in the Twelve Steps devotional reading plan in this Bible have been adapted from the Twelve Steps of Alcoholics Anonymous.

THE TWELVE STEPS OF ALCOHOLICS ANONYMOUS

1. We admitted we were powerless over alcohol—that our lives had become unmanageable.
2. Came to believe that a Power greater than ourselves could restore us to sanity.
3. Made a decision to turn our will and our lives over to the care of God *as we understood Him.*
4. Made a searching and fearless moral inventory of ourselves.
5. Admitted to God, to ourselves and to another human being the exact nature of our wrongs.
6. Were entirely ready to have God remove all these defects of character.
7. Humbly asked Him to remove our shortcomings.
8. Made a list of all persons we had harmed, and became willing to make amends to them all.
9. Made direct amends to such people wherever possible, except when to do so would injure them or others.
10. Continued to take personal inventory and when we were wrong promptly admitted it.
11. Sought through prayer and meditation to improve our conscious contact with God, *as we understood Him,* praying only for knowledge of His will for us and the power to carry that out.
12. Having had a spiritual awakening as the result of these steps, we tried to carry this message to alcoholics, and to practice these principles in all our affairs.

The Twelve Steps are reprinted and adapted with permission of Alcoholics Anonymous World Services, Inc. Permission to reprint and adapt the Twelve Steps does not mean that AA has reviewed or approved the contents of this publication, nor that AA agrees with the views expressed herein. AA is a program of recovery from alcoholism—use of the Twelve Steps in connection with programs and activities which are patterned after AA, but which address other problems, does not imply otherwise.

CONTRIBUTORS

Executive Editors
David A. Stoop
Stephen A. Arterburn

Associate Editors
A. Boyd Luter
Connie Neal

Managing Editor
Mark R. Norton

Editorial Staff
Derrick Blanchette
Meg Diehl
Diane Eble
Betsy Elliott
Dietrich Gruen
Lucille Leonard
Phyllis LePeau
Daryl Lucas
Judith Morse
Kathy Stinnette
Ramona Tucker
Sally van der Graaff
Esther Waldrop
Karen Walker
Wightman Weese

Production Staff
Dan Beery
Linda Oswald
Lois Rusch
Julee Schwarzburg

Graphic Designer
Timothy R. Botts

Writers
Donald E. Anderson
Shelley M. Chapin
R. Tony Cothren
Shelly O. Cunningham
Barry C. Davis
Harold Dollar
Joseph M. Espinoza
Thomas J. Finley
William J. Gaultiere
Ronald N. Glass
Daniel M. Hahn
Eric Hoey
Mark W. Hoffman
John C. Hutchison
Tommy A. Jarrett
Stephen M. Johnson
G. Ted Martinez
Kathy McReynolds
V. Eric Nachtrieb
Stephen L. Newman
T. Ken Oberholtzer
Scott B. Rae
Richard O. Rigsby
Jane E. Rodgers
Walter B. Russell
Richard F. Travis

USER'S GUIDE

The Holy Bible is a book about recovery. It records how the world began and how God created it to be good. Then it tells us about the beginning of sin— about the first time people decided to reject God's plan. It spells out the fatal consequences that result from rejecting God's program. But the Bible doesn't leave us in despair. It reveals a plan for recovery and the source of the power to accomplish it. It provides us with the only pathway to wholeness— God's program for reconciliation and healing. Each feature in *The Life Recovery Bible* leads its readers to the powerful resources for recovery found in the Holy Scriptures:

DEVOTIONAL
READING PLANS

Each devotional is set near the Scripture it comments on and directs the reader to the next devotional in the reading chain.

* The **Twelve Step Devotional Reading Plan** includes eighty-four Bible-based devotionals built around the Twelve Steps.
For the first devotional in this reading plan, turn to page 17.

* The **Recovery Principle Devotional Reading Plan** is composed of fifty-six Bible-based devotionals shaped around principles important in the recovery process.
For the first devotional in this reading plan, turn to page 3.

* The **Serenity Prayer Devotional Reading Plan** is made up of thirty Bible-based devotionals related to the Serenity Prayer.
For the first devotional in this reading plan, turn to page 21.

RECOVERY PROFILES

In this feature over sixty individuals and relationships are profiled and important recovery lessons are drawn from their lives. For an example of this feature, turn to page 5.

INTRODUCTORY MATERIAL FOR BIBLE BOOKS

Each book of the Bible is preceded by a number of helpful features.

* **Book Introductions** present the content and themes from the standpoint of recovery.
* **The Big Picture** gives a panoramic view of the book in outline form.
* **The Bottom Line** provides vital historical information for the book.
* **Recovery Themes** presents and discusses important themes for people in recovery.

Turn to pages 1 and 2 for these introductory features.

RECOVERY COMMENTARY NOTES

The Bible text is supported by numerous **Recovery Notes** that pinpoint passages and thoughts important to recovery. This feature can be found at the foot of most pages.

* Additional commentary material is provided in the **Recovery Reflections** that follow many of the Bible books. Here, notes are topically arranged and reflect back on the preceding book.

Turn to page 64 for an example of this feature.

INDEXES

The **Life Recovery Topical Index** guides the reader to the important notes, profiles, devotionals, and recovery themes related to more than a hundred terms important to issues in the recovery process.

* The **Index to Recovery Profiles** alphabetically lists and locates the sixty Relationship Profiles that appear in this Bible.
* The **Index to Twelve Step Devotionals** lists and locates the eighty-four Twelve Step devotionals.
* The **Index to Recovery Principle Devotionals** lists and locates the fifty-six recovery principle devotionals.
* The **Index to Serenity Prayer Devotionals** lists and locates the thirty Serenity Prayer devotionals.
* The **Index to Recovery Reflections** lists and locates the various topics discussed in the Reflections feature of this Bible.

These indexes do not appear in this booklet.

PREFACE

THE BIBLE is the greatest book on recovery ever written. In its pages, we watch as God sets out a plan for the recovery of his broken people and creation. We meet numerous individuals whose hurting lives are mended through the wisdom and power of God. We meet the God who is waiting with arms outstretched for all of us to turn back to him, seek after his ways, and recover the wonderful plan he has for us.

Many of us are just waking up to the fact that recovery is an essential part of life for everyone. It is the simple but challenging process of daily seeking God's will for our life instead of demanding to go our own way. It is allowing God to do for us what we cannot do for ourselves, while also taking the steps necessary to draw closer to our Creator and Redeemer. It is a process of allowing God to heal our wounded soul so we can help others in the process of healing. All of us need to take part in this process; it is an inherent part of being human.

Let us set out together on a journey toward healing and newfound strength. Not strength found within ourselves, but strength found through trusting God and allowing him to direct our decisions and plans. This journey will take us through the Twelve Steps and other materials designed to help us focus on the powerful provisions God offers for recovery. *The Life Recovery Bible* will enrich our experience and expand our understanding of the God who loves us and sent his Son to die that we might be made whole.

Without God, there is no recovery, only disappointing substitutions and repeated failure. We pray that the resources within these pages will help us all better understand who God is and how he wants to heal our brokenness and set us on the path toward wholeness.

GENESIS

THE BIG PICTURE

A. GOD SETS THE STAGE (1:1–11:32)
1. Formation of the Universe (1:1–2:25)
   a. God creates matter, energy, and the natural order (1:1–2:3)
   b. God prepares pristine surroundings for the first family (2:4-25)
2. Fall of the Human Race (3:1–3:24)
   a. Commission of sin (3:1-8)
   b. Curse on sin (3:9-24)
3. Failure of Society (4:1–9:29)
   a. Failure of humankind (4:1–6:22)
   b. Flood of judgment (7:1–9:29)
4. Folly of Rebellion (10:1–11:32)
   a. Dispersal of the people (10:1-32)
   b. Disobedience of the people (11:1-32)

B. GOD CHOOSES THE PLAYERS (12:1–50:26)
1. Abraham (12:1–25:18)
2. Isaac (25:19–27:46)
3. Jacob (28:1–36:43)
4. Joseph (37:1–50:26)

The book of Genesis is a book of beginnings. It records how the world began and how God created it to be good. It tells us about the first people and how God made them to be excellent. But then it tells us about the beginning of sin—about the first time people decided to reject the program God had laid out for them. It records the first days of shame and of covering up. It records the beginning of our separation from God, each other, and the world God gave us.

We will see how people with perfect health, living in a perfect environment, rebelled against God. And we will see the consequences of their rebellion. We are given intimate glimpses of individuals dominated by hatred, drunkenness, lust, unhealthy family relationships, money, cheating, irresponsibility, dishonesty, jealousy, violence, and other difficulties.

But the book of Genesis doesn't leave us in despair. It tells us of yet another beginning. It records how God chose a man named Abraham to father a special nation. And through this nation would come the solution for our separation from God, each other, and the world God gave us. Genesis begins the story of how God began his work of healing broken humanity—a healing to be expressed in the laws he would give his people, and culminating in the coming of Jesus, the promised Messiah.

The book of Genesis reminds us of where all our problems began. It spells out the fatal consequences of rejecting God's program. But it also begins the agelong story of God's unstoppable love for the human race. Through this book we will discover that the only pathway to spiritual wholeness is in following God's program.

THE BOTTOM LINE

PURPOSE: To tell us about the beginning of things, including human opportunities and difficulties, and to demonstrate that God's solutions are the only ones that work. AUTHOR: Moses. AUDIENCE: The people of Israel. DATE WRITTEN: Chapters 1–11 deal with the undateable past; the events of chapters 12–50 are to be dated between about 2000 and 1800 B.C. The book was probably written shortly after 1445 B.C. SETTING: Mesopotamia, then Canaan, finally Egypt. KEY VERSE: "And Abram believed God; then God considered him righteous on account of his faith" (15:6). KEY EVENTS: Creation, the Fall, the Flood, the Tower of Babel. KEY PEOPLE: Abraham, Isaac, Jacob, Joseph.

RECOVERY THEMES

A Good Creation: Everything about God's creation was described as being good except the fact that Adam was alone. In fact, Adam's isolation is the only thing in the first two chapters of Genesis that God considered to be a problem. When God created a partner for man, then he was pleased with everything in his creation. Because God was pleased with what he created, he stayed involved, even after Adam and Eve disobeyed him. In fact, ever since the Fall God has been seeking to make things right again. Our sinfulness always leads us away from God and distorts the way God created us to be. But our recovery always involves growth toward God's original ideal for the human race. As we progress in recovery, we take part in God's re-creation of our fallen world.

A Ruined World: Adam and Eve's disobedience affected all of God's creation. The idyllic world of the garden was gone forever, and life became a struggle. Our futile attempts to avoid the realities of a ruined world have led us into all kinds of destructive behaviors. Recovery begins when we squarely face the broken realities of our world—its daily struggles and hardships. Once we have done this, we have started down the road of recovery. We have entered the spiritual arena where battles are fought to regain what has been lost.

Promises of Healing: The book of Genesis presents us with a series of "new beginnings" that come out of the ruin of our sinfulness. In the original Fall, God promised hope and healing for us when he told the serpent that the offspring of the woman would crush his head. When people generally continued to disobey, God sent the Flood as judgment for their sinfulness. After the Flood, God again promised victory and represented that promise with a rainbow. Then the human race rejected God again, building a great tower as a memorial of their pride. In response, God confused their languages, further fragmenting society. Then God chose a man named Abram and promised to bless all nations of the world through his offspring. Each time that human sin brought ruin, God promised victory and recovery in the face of it.

Hope for Reconciliation: As people began to experience the terrible consequences of their disobedience, God didn't leave them to figure out a plan for recovery all alone. He didn't leave a long list of principles or rules to follow that would repair their damaged relationships. Instead, God always worked with people on a very personal level in the recovery process. As we enter into the recovery process, we find it to be relational in character. It requires us to seek reconciliation with people close to us; and this includes God. In Genesis, God modeled this pattern for us time and again. He chose certain individuals and worked patiently in their lives, reconciling them with the people around them.

CHAPTER 1
God Creates a Good World
When God began creating the heavens and the earth, ²the earth was a shapeless, chaotic mass, with the Spirit of God brooding over the dark vapors.

³Then God said, "Let there be light." And light appeared. ⁴,⁵And God was pleased with it and divided the light from the darkness. He called the light "daytime," and the darkness "nighttime." Together they formed the first day.

⁶And God said, "Let the vapors separate to form the sky above and the oceans below."

⁷,⁸So God made the sky, dividing the vapor above from the water below. This all happened on the second day.

⁹,¹⁰Then God said, "Let the water beneath the sky be gathered into oceans so that the dry land will emerge." And so it was. Then God named the dry land "earth," and the water "seas." And God was pleased. ¹¹,¹²And he said, "Let the earth burst forth with every sort of grass and seed-bearing plant, and fruit trees with seeds inside the fruit, so that these seeds will produce the kinds of plants and fruits they came from." And so it was, and God was pleased. ¹³This all occurred on the third day.

1:4 God was pleased with his creation. He declared that it was good. God stopped now and then to approve of what he designed and created (1:4-5, 9-10, 11-12, 18, 21-22, 25, 31). Many of our problems and dependencies result from the misuse of God's good creation. Our recovery may involve discovering the good things that we have misused and learning how to enjoy them in the way God intended.
1:24 The phrase "And so it was" (also in 1:9-12, 14-15) shows us that God's creative activity was done in complete conformity to the specifications he had originally intended. God accomplishes his will with certainty and precision. It should reassure us to know that God's good desires for us can be accomplished with the same certainty.
2:2-3 This is the first mention of Sabbath rest—one day of rest in seven. By his example God encourages us to designate a portion of our life to rest and spiritual rejuvenation. Without proper rest, it is very difficult to deal with the other matters in our life, especially our progress in recovery.

^{14,15}Then God said, "Let bright lights appear in the sky to give light to the earth and to identify the day and the night; they shall bring about the seasons on the earth, and mark the days and years." And so it was. ¹⁶For God had made two huge lights, the sun and moon, to shine down upon the earth—the larger one, the sun, to preside over the day and the smaller one, the moon, to preside through the night; he had also made the stars. ¹⁷And God set them in the sky to light the earth, ¹⁸and to preside over the day and night, and to divide the light from the darkness. And God was pleased. ¹⁹This all happened on the fourth day.

²⁰Then God said, "Let the waters teem with fish and other life, and let the skies be filled with birds of every kind." ^{21,22}So God created great sea animals, and every sort of fish and every kind of bird. And God looked at them with pleasure, and blessed them all. "Multiply and stock the oceans," he told them, and to the birds he said, "Let your numbers increase. Fill the earth!" ²³That ended the fifth day.

²⁴And God said, "Let the earth bring forth every kind of animal—cattle and reptiles and wildlife of every kind." And so it was. ²⁵God made all sorts of wild animals and cattle and reptiles. And God was pleased with what he had done.

²⁶Then God said, "Let us make a man—someone like ourselves, to be the master of all life upon the earth and in the skies and in the seas."

²⁷So God made man like his Maker.
Like God did God make man;
Man and maid did he make them.

²⁸And God blessed them and told them, "Multiply and fill the earth and subdue it; you are masters of the fish and birds and all the animals. ²⁹And look! I have given you the seed-bearing plants throughout the earth and all the fruit trees for your food. ³⁰And I've given all the grass and plants to the animals and birds for their food." ³¹Then God looked over all that he had made, and it was excellent in every way. This ended the sixth day.

CHAPTER 2
Now at last the heavens and earth were successfully completed, with all that they contained. ²So on the seventh day, having finished his task, God ceased from this work he had been doing, ³and God blessed the seventh day and declared it holy, because it

▶ The recovery principle devotional reading plan begins here.

Self-perception

READ GENESIS 1:26-31

If we have lived in bondage to our compulsive behaviors for a while, we probably see more bad inside us than good. Many of us tend to see life in terms of all or nothing. As a result, we probably think of ourself as being all bad. But in recovery, we need a balanced understanding of ourself. We need to see that along with our bad points we have also been gifted with strengths. It's not an either/or proposition. A balanced view of ourself will help us better understand our shortcomings while also giving us greater hope in our potential.

At the end of the fifth day of creation God had made everything except for the first man and woman. The Bible tells us that when he had finished, "God was pleased with what he had done." Then God created the first man and woman. "So God made man like his Maker. Like God did God make man. . . . And God blessed them and told them, 'Multiply and fill the earth and subdue it; you are masters of the fish and birds and all the animals.' . . . Then God looked over all that he had made, and it was excellent in every way" (Genesis 1:25, 27-31).

God made a distinction between his estimation of the human race and the rest of creation. God made us in his very image, with capacities far beyond those of mere animals. God was (and is) excited about us! He gave us abilities and responsibilities to reflect his own nature in all of creation. When he created us, he was proud of what he made!

Although we have a sinful nature which came after the Fall, we also must remember that we were created in the likeness of God. There's an excellence and dignity inherent in being human that should cause us to ponder our potential for good as well as bad. *Turn to page 25, Genesis 22.*

was the day when he ceased this work of creation.

⁴Here is a summary of the events in the creation of the heavens and earth when the Lord God made them.

⁵There were no plants or grain sprouting up across the earth at first, for the Lord God hadn't sent any rain; nor was there anyone to farm the soil. ⁶(However, water welled up from the ground at certain places and flowed across the land.)

God Creates Adam and Eve
⁷The time came when the Lord God formed a man's body from the dust of the ground and breathed into it the breath of life. And man became a living person.

⁸Then the Lord God planted a garden in Eden, to the east, and placed in the garden the man he had formed. ⁹The Lord God planted all sorts of beautiful trees there in the garden, trees producing the choicest of fruit. At the center of the garden he placed the Tree of Life, and also the Tree of Conscience, giving knowledge of Good and Bad. ¹⁰A river from the land of Eden flowed through the garden to water it; afterwards the river divided into four branches. ¹¹,¹²One of these was named the Pishon; it winds across the entire length of the land of Havilah, where nuggets of pure gold are found, also beautiful bdellium and even lapis lazuli. ¹³The second branch is called the Gihon, crossing the entire length of the land of Cush. ¹⁴The third branch is the Tigris, which flows to the east of the city of Asher. And the fourth is the Euphrates.

¹⁵The Lord God placed the man in the Garden of Eden as its gardener, to tend and care for it. ¹⁶,¹⁷But the Lord God gave the man this warning: "You may eat any fruit in the garden except fruit from the Tree of Conscience—for

its fruit will open your eyes to make you aware of right and wrong, good and bad. If you eat its fruit, you will be doomed to die."

¹⁸And the Lord God said, "It isn't good for man to be alone; I will make a companion for him, a helper suited to his needs." ¹⁹,²⁰So the Lord God formed from the soil every kind of animal and bird, and brought them to the man to see what he would call them; and whatever he called them, that was their name. But still there was no proper helper for the man. ²¹Then the Lord God caused the man to fall into a deep sleep, and took one of his ribs and closed up the place from which he had removed it, ²²and made the rib into a woman, and brought her to the man.

²³"This is it!" Adam exclaimed. "She is part of my own bone and flesh! Her name is 'woman' because she was taken out of a man." ²⁴This explains why a man leaves his father and mother and is joined to his wife in such a way that the two become one person. ²⁵Now although the man and his wife were both naked, neither of them was embarrassed or ashamed.

CHAPTER 3
Adam and Eve Sin
The serpent was the craftiest of all the creatures the Lord God had made. So the serpent came to the woman. "Really?" he asked. "*None* of the fruit in the garden? God says you mustn't eat *any* of it?"

²,³"Of course we may eat it," the woman told him. "It's only the fruit from the tree at the *center* of the garden that we are not to eat. God says we mustn't eat it or even touch it, or we will die."

⁴"That's a lie!" the serpent hissed. "You'll not die! ⁵God knows very well that the instant

2:8-14 God provided a perfect environment for the first people. We often blame our outward circumstances for our difficulties. It is important to note here that in spite of their ideal surroundings, our first parents fell—they failed. Although the environment we live in can certainly add to our problems, it is never entirely at fault. We need to take responsibility for our own mistakes and failures.
3:1-5 The account here pictures for us the process of temptation. The serpent offered something that had been forbidden by God as a very attractive option. The serpent also caused Eve to doubt God and the truth of his Word. During the debate, Eve offered some halfhearted opposition, but her growing doubt in God weakened her resolve. In the end she gave in. Satan strengthened his temptation by weakening Eve's faith in God. Staying close to God and maintaining our faith in him will weaken the power of temptation in our life.
3:12-13 When Adam was questioned, notice that he blamed the woman for his problem. He even backhandedly blamed God by reminding God that he was the one who gave him the woman in the first place. Then Eve blamed the serpent for the problem. Passing the buck is a standard human response to guilt. But our recovery requires that we take a thorough inventory of our life, accepting responsibility for everything we have done or failed to do.

ADAM & EVE

It was an ideal situation: a man and his wife living harmoniously together in a lush, beautiful garden that God had created for their pleasure. They enjoyed perfect relationships with God and with each other. But when Eve submitted to temptation, they overstepped their God-given boundaries and plunged the human race into sin. Harmony was broken. Shame and guilt penetrated their lives and created an invisible barrier between them and God. The consequences of their disobedience and lack of self-control are with us to this day.

Adam and Eve knew that they had gone against God's plan—a plan that was created with their best interests in mind. And the consequences of their sin followed immediately. Right away they became afraid of the God who loved them so much, and they hid from his presence. They also became ashamed of their nakedness and set out to cover themselves. The relationship between the man and his wife began to show cracks and strains. Accusations were made. Blame was shifted. Neither of them wanted to be held accountable. They refused to admit that they were wrong. Needless to say, their relationship was damaged. Their sin had separated them from each other and from God.

But the story doesn't end there. Adam and Eve stayed together in spite of the shame and guilt they felt. Their lives were marred by sin and scarred by wounds inflicted on one another. However, they faced the reality that life had to go on and began to build a new life together. And by love, commitment, and the grace of God, they persevered through life's trials.

The story of Adam and Eve is found in the opening chapters of Genesis. Adam and/or Eve are also mentioned in 1 Chronicles 1:1; Romans 5:12-21; 1 Corinthians 15:22, 45-47; 2 Corinthians 11:3; and 1 Timothy 2:13-15.

STRENGTHS AND ACCOMPLISHMENTS:
- They were the parents of the entire human race.
- They were committed to each other through the trials they faced.
- Their story provides us with the first illustration of God's grace.

WEAKNESSES AND MISTAKES:
- They were disobedient to the plan that God had revealed to them.
- They were not willing to take responsibility for their sin.
- They made excuses rather than admitting the truth.
- They brought sin into the world and passed it on to their descendants.

LESSONS FROM THEIR LIVES:
- A good marriage requires love and commitment even through the tough times.
- Relationships that accept God's grace and forgiveness persevere through life's difficulties.
- Complacency is a breeding ground for temptation—be on guard against Satan's schemes.
- The mistakes of parents are often passed on to their descendants.

KEY VERSE:
"Then God said, 'Let us make a man—someone like ourselves, to be the master of all life upon the earth and in the skies and in the seas.' So God made man like his Maker. Like God did God make man; man and maid did he make them" (Genesis 1:26-27).

---

you eat it you will become like him, for your eyes will be opened—you will be able to distinguish good from evil!"

⁶The woman was convinced. How lovely and fresh looking it was! And it would make her so wise! So she ate some of the fruit and gave some to her husband, and he ate it too. ⁷And as they ate it, suddenly they became aware of their nakedness, and were embarrassed. So they strung fig leaves together to cover themselves around the hips.

⁸That evening they heard the sound of the Lord God walking in the garden; and they hid themselves among the trees. ⁹The Lord God called to Adam, "Why are you hiding?"

¹⁰And Adam replied, "I heard you coming and didn't want you to see me naked. So I hid."

¹¹"Who told you you were naked?" the Lord God asked. "Have you eaten fruit from the tree I warned you about?"

¹²"Yes," Adam admitted, "but it was the woman you gave me who brought me some, and I ate it."

¹³Then the Lord God asked the woman, "How could you do such a thing?"

"The serpent tricked me," she replied.

¹⁴So the Lord God said to the serpent, "This is your punishment: You are singled out from among all the domestic and wild animals of the whole earth—to be cursed. You shall grovel in the dust as long as you live, crawling along on your belly. ¹⁵From now on you and the woman will be enemies, as will your offspring and hers. You will strike his heel, but he will crush your head."

¹⁶Then God said to the woman, "You shall bear children in intense pain and suffering; yet even so, you shall welcome your husband's affections, and he shall be your master."

¹⁷And to Adam, God said, "Because you listened to your wife and ate the fruit when I told you not to, I have placed a curse upon the soil. All your life you will struggle to extract a living from it. ¹⁸It will grow thorns and thistles for you, and you shall eat its grasses. ¹⁹All your life you will sweat to master it, until your dying day. Then you will return to the ground from which you came. For you were made from the ground, and to the ground you will return."

²⁰The man named his wife Eve (meaning "The life-giving one"), for he said, "She shall become the mother of all mankind"; ²¹and the Lord God clothed Adam and his wife with garments made from skins of animals.

²²Then the Lord said, "Now that the man has become as we are, knowing good from bad, what if he eats the fruit of the Tree of Life and lives forever?" ²³So the Lord God banished him forever from the Garden of Eden, and sent him out to farm the ground from which he had been taken. ²⁴Thus God expelled him, and placed mighty angels at the east of the Garden of Eden, with a flaming sword to guard the entrance to the Tree of Life.

CHAPTER 4
Cain Murders Abel

Then Adam had sexual intercourse with Eve his wife, and she conceived and gave birth to a son, Cain (meaning "I have created"). For, as she said, "With God's help, I have created a man!" ²Her next child was his brother, Abel.

Abel became a shepherd, while Cain was a farmer. ³At harvest time Cain brought the Lord a gift of his farm produce, ⁴and Abel brought the fatty cuts of meat from his best lambs, and presented them to the Lord. And the Lord accepted Abel's offering, ⁵but not Cain's. This made Cain both dejected and very angry, and his face grew dark with fury.

⁶"Why are you angry?" the Lord asked him. "Why is your face so dark with rage? ⁷It can be bright with joy if you will do what you should! But if you refuse to obey, watch out. Sin is waiting to attack you, longing to destroy you. But you can conquer it!"

⁸One day Cain suggested to his brother, "Let's go out into the fields." And while they were together there, Cain attacked and killed his brother.

⁹But afterwards the Lord asked Cain, "Where is your brother? Where is Abel?"

"How should I know?" Cain retorted. "Am I supposed to keep track of him wherever he goes?"

¹⁰But the Lord said, "Your brother's blood calls to me from the ground. What have you done? ¹¹You are hereby banished from this ground which you have defiled with your brother's blood. ¹²No longer will it yield crops for you, even if you toil on it forever! From now on you will be a fugitive and a tramp upon the earth, wandering from place to place."

3:21 The first death did occur on the day of Adam's sin, but it was the death of an animal to provide a covering for Adam and Eve's nakedness. God's immediate provision for sin was the slaying of an innocent substitute to provide skins to clothe the guilty couple. The clothing they wore must have served as a reminder—engraving the sight of the dying animal in their minds—a picture of the terrible consequences of their sin. As we recognize the suffering we may have caused others, we also are reminded of the consequences of rejecting God's program for our life.

4:6-7 When God rejected Cain's offering, Cain reacted first with disappointment, but then with anger. God did not reject Cain for his strong feelings, but offered him an opportunity for a new start. How sad that Cain refused this second chance and went out instead to kill his brother. We need to be careful when we face obstacles to our recovery. We need to carefully weigh the strong feelings we encounter before acting on them. If we don't, we may be passing up an excellent opportunity for a fresh start. God is not put off by our strong feelings. Our recovery is based on God's grace, which always offers us an opportunity to begin again.

4:15 The "mark of Cain" was not, as some have taught, a badge of guilt. It was a sign that God gave to Cain for his protection. Even after Cain's great failure, God desired to protect him from harm. Many of us look back and marvel at how God protected us before we began our recovery. He wants us to be restored and often protects us in the midst of evil so that we are not destroyed. Even after our greatest failures, our gracious God desires only our healing and recovery.

4:19-24 Some people insist that the human race is developing and becoming better and better. When we compare Lamech with his ancestor Cain, it is obvious that the trend usually goes in the opposite direction. Without God's help, we only get worse. It is only by following God's program and receiving his grace that we can hope to escape the natural slide toward pain and destruction.

¹³Cain replied to the Lord, "My punishment is greater than I can bear. ¹⁴For you have banished me from my farm and from you, and made me a fugitive and a tramp; and everyone who sees me will try to kill me."

¹⁵The Lord replied, "They won't kill you, for I will give seven times your punishment to anyone who does." Then the Lord put an identifying mark on Cain as a warning not to kill him. ¹⁶So Cain went out from the presence of the Lord and settled in the land of Nod, east of Eden.

Cain's Family
¹⁷Then Cain's wife conceived and presented him with a baby son named Enoch; so when Cain founded a city, he named it Enoch, after his son.

¹⁸Enoch was the father of Irad; Irad was the father of Mehujael; Mehujael was the father of Methusael; Methusael was the father of Lamech;

¹⁹Lamech married two wives—Adah and Zillah. ²⁰To Adah was born a baby named Jabal. He became the first of the cattlemen and those living in tents. ²¹His brother's name was Jubal, the first musician—the inventor of the harp and flute. ²²To Lamech's other wife, Zillah, was born Tubal-cain. He opened the first foundry forging instruments of bronze and iron.

²³One day Lamech said to Adah and Zillah, "Listen to me, my wives. I have killed a youth who attacked and wounded me. ²⁴If anyone who kills Cain will be punished seven times, anyone taking revenge against me for killing that youth should be punished seventy-seven times!"

Adam's Family
²⁵Later on Eve gave birth to another son and named him Seth (meaning "Granted"); for, as Eve put it, "God has granted me another son for the one Cain killed." ²⁶When Seth grew up, he had a son and named him Enosh. It was during his lifetime that men first began to call themselves "the Lord's people."

CHAPTER 5
Here is a list of some of the descendants of Adam—the man who was like God from the day of his creation. ²God created man and woman and blessed them, and called them Man from the start.

³⁻⁵*Adam:* Adam was 130 years old when his son Seth was born, the very image of his father in every way. After Seth was born,

Coming out of Hiding
BIBLE READING: Genesis 3:6-13
We made a searching and fearless moral inventory of ourselves.
Many of us have spent our life in a state of hiding, ashamed of who we are inside. We may hide by living a double life, using our drug of choice to make us feel like someone else, or by self-righteously setting ourselves above others. Step Four involves uncovering the things we have been hiding, even from ourselves.

After Adam and Eve disobeyed God, "suddenly they became aware of their nakedness, and were embarrassed. So they strung fig leaves together to cover themselves around the hips. . . . The Lord God called to Adam, 'Why are you hiding?' And Adam replied, 'I heard you coming and didn't want you to see me naked. So I hid'" (Genesis 3:7-10). Human beings have been covering up and hiding ever since!

Jesus consistently confronted the religious leaders for their hypocrisy. The word *hypocrite* describes a person who pretends to have virtues or qualities that he really doesn't have. One time Jesus said to them, "Hypocrites! You are so careful to polish the outside of the cup, but the inside is foul with extortion and greed. . . . First cleanse the inside of the cup, and then the whole cup will be clean" (Matthew 23:25-26).

When the real person inside comes out of hiding, we will have to deal with some dirt! Making this inventory is a good way to "cleanse the inside"; and some of that cleansing may involve bathing our life with tears. It is only by uncovering the hidden parts of ourselves that we will be able to change the outer person, including our addictive/compulsive behaviors. *Turn to page 541, Nehemiah 8.*

Adam lived another 800 years, producing sons and daughters, and died at the age of 930.

⁶⁻⁸*Seth:* Seth was 105 years old when his son Enosh was born. Afterwards he lived another 807 years, producing sons and daughters, and died at the age of 912.

⁹⁻¹¹*Enosh:* Enosh was ninety years old when his son Kenan was born. Afterwards he lived another 815 years, producing sons and daughters, and died at the age of 905.

¹²⁻¹⁴*Kenan:* Kenan was seventy years old when his son Mahalalel was born. Afterwards he lived another 840 years, producing sons and daughters, and died at the age of 910.

¹⁵⁻¹⁷*Mahalalel:* Mahalalel was sixty-five years old when his son Jared was born. Afterwards he lived 830 years, producing sons and daughters, and died at the age of 895.

¹⁸⁻²⁰*Jared:* Jared was 162 years old when his son Enoch was born. Afterwards he lived another 800 years, producing sons and daughters, and died at the age of 962.

²¹⁻²⁴*Enoch:* Enoch was sixty-five years old when his son Methuselah was born. Afterwards he lived another 300 years in fellowship with God, and produced sons and daughters; then, when he was 365, and in constant touch with God, he disappeared, for God took him!

²⁵⁻²⁷*Methuselah:* Methuselah was 187 years old when his son Lamech was born; afterwards he lived another 782 years, producing sons and daughters, and died at the age of 969.

²⁸⁻³¹*Lamech:* Lamech was 182 years old when his son Noah was born. Lamech named him Noah (meaning "Relief") because he said, "He will bring us relief from the hard work of farming this ground which God has cursed." Afterwards Lamech lived 595 years, producing sons and daughters, and died at the age of 777.

³²*Noah:* Noah was 500 years old and had three sons, Shem, Ham, and Japheth.

CHAPTER 6
The People Turn from God
Now a population explosion took place upon the earth. It was at this time that beings from the spirit world looked upon the beautiful earth women and took any they desired to be their wives. ³Then Jehovah said, "My Spirit must not forever be disgraced in man, wholly evil as he is. I will give him 120 years to mend his ways."

⁴In those days, and even afterwards, when the evil beings from the spirit world were sexually involved with human women, their children became giants, of whom so many legends are told. ⁵When the Lord God saw the extent of human wickedness, and that the trend and direction of men's lives were only towards evil, ⁶he was sorry he had made them. It broke his heart.

⁷And he said, "I will blot out from the face of the earth all mankind that I created. Yes, and the animals too, and the reptiles and the birds. For I am sorry I made them."

Noah Obeys God
⁸But Noah was a pleasure to the Lord. Here is the story of Noah:⁹,¹⁰He was the only truly righteous man living on the earth at that

---

5:1-32 This chapter has often been called the obituary column. Its recurring refrain is "and [he] died . . . and [he] died . . . and [he] died." Although physical death did not occur on the day Adam sinned, it did eventually come. Adam had reestablished his relationship with God, but the physical consequences of his sin could not be avoided forever. We may hope that after reestablishing our relationship with God, our troubles will be over. But a relationship with God rarely frees us from the consequences of past sin. The consequences usually catch up with us sooner or later. But if we suffer for past mistakes, we can know that God will be with us each step of the way.
5:21-24 Little is said about the spiritual state of these patriarchs of the human race. But the account of Enoch's life provides us with a bright spot in this otherwise dismal chapter. Enoch was said to be "in constant touch with God." His life should give us hope. He wasn't trapped by the mistakes or apathy of his peers and ancestors. Instead, he made a new start. And he did it by constantly walking with God.
6:3 In spite of the sinfulness of the human race, God still acted graciously toward them. He gave them 120 years to mend their ways and turn to him. God always gives ample warning before he sends judgment. He does this to give us time to change our ways. He wants us to experience the advantages of a life lived according to his plans and purposes. He never desires our destruction.
6:8-10 God did not destroy the righteous with the wicked. These verses are another statement of God's grace. God extended grace to Noah and his family. Noah knew Enoch's secret. He lived his life in constant fellowship with God. He broke the mold set by his ancestors and neighbors by drawing close to God. As a result, Noah lived through the flood and became the second father of the human race.

CAIN & ABEL

How often parents of two children have been heard to exclaim, "There have *never* been two children who were more different!" Adam and Eve could well have been the originators of that comment. Cain apparently felt himself to be in direct competition with Abel. This led to a rivalry that was never resolved, resulting in a major tragedy.

Cain became a farmer and Abel a shepherd. It was their offerings, however, not their occupations, that revealed the true nature of their character. Abel did things God's way, following his requirements. He is called "righteous" in Matthew 23:35, and Hebrews 11:4 says his offering was made by faith. Cain, on the other hand, did things his own way. Jude suggests that his "way" was that of rebellion (Jude 1:11). Cain brought an offering of produce from his gardens, while Abel brought the fatty cuts of meat from his best lambs.

Abel's altar was ugly; every sense was assaulted by the bloody carcass lying across it. But the blood was a part of God's plan according to Hebrews 12:24. Cain's offering had the potential of being beautiful. Picture fresh produce, just out of the garden—fruits, vegetables, flowers, and grain—probably lovingly and artistically arranged. Perhaps Cain wanted to be accepted by God on the basis of his own merits. He may not have been willing to have a relationship with God based on a bloody sacrifice. When God accepted Abel's offering and rejected Cain's, Cain became angry. But God did not reject him for his anger. Even at that point, God reasoned with him. He offered Cain another opportunity to change his mind and accept divine grace; but still Cain refused. Jealous of Abel whose offering had been accepted and raging because God had rejected his own, Cain murdered his brother.

Cain tried to hide his terrible deed, but God was not fooled. God confronted Cain with the murder and assigned the consequence of lifelong exile. Cain spent the rest of his life as an alien, wandering in lands far from his family. But even in exile God protected him; God placed his mark upon Cain to protect him from being killed.

STRENGTHS AND ACCOMPLISHMENTS:
- Abel was obedient to God.
- Abel is the first hero mentioned in the "Gallery of Faith" in Hebrews 11.
- Both sons developed skills and worked hard in the occupations they chose.

WEAKNESSES AND MISTAKES:
- Cain insisted on doing things his own way.
- When rejected, Cain reacted with rage.
- Cain allowed his rage to lead him to commit the first murder.

LESSONS FROM THEIR LIVES:
- Our righteousness is based on our willingness to follow God's program by faith.
- Feeling anger does not separate us from God unless we express it in destructive ways.
- Though we may try to hide our sins for a time, God's justice will prevail.

KEY VERSE:
"It was by faith that Abel obeyed God and brought an offering that pleased God more than Cain's offering did. God accepted Abel and proved it by accepting his gift; and though Abel is long dead, we can still learn lessons from him about trusting God" (Hebrews 11:4).

The account of Cain and Abel is given in Genesis 4. Both also are mentioned in Hebrews 11:4 and 1 John 3:12. Cain alone is referred to in Jude 1:11; Abel is spoken of in Matthew 23:35; Luke 11:51; and Hebrews 12:24.

---

time. He tried always to conduct his affairs according to God's will. And he had three sons—Shem, Ham, and Japheth.

[11]Meanwhile, the crime rate was rising rapidly across the earth, and, as seen by God, the world was rotten to the core.

[12,13]As God observed how bad it was, and saw that all mankind was vicious and depraved, he said to Noah, "I have decided to destroy all mankind; for the earth is filled with crime because of man. Yes, I will destroy mankind from the earth. [14]Make a boat from resinous wood, sealing it with tar; and construct decks and stalls throughout the ship. [15]Make it 450 feet long, 75 feet wide, and 45 feet high. [16]Construct a skylight all the way around the ship, eighteen inches below the roof; and make three decks inside the boat—a bottom, middle, and upper deck—and put a door in the side.

[17]"Look! I am going to cover the earth with a flood and destroy every living being—everything in which there is the breath of life. All will die. [18]But I promise to keep you safe in the

ship, with your wife and your sons and their wives. [19,20]Bring a pair of every animal—a male and a female—into the boat with you, to keep them alive through the flood. Bring in a pair of each kind of bird and animal and reptile. [21]Store away in the boat all the food that they and you will need." [22]And Noah did everything as God commanded him.

CHAPTER 7
Finally the day came when the Lord said to Noah, "Go into the boat with all your family, for among all the people of the earth, I consider you alone to be righteous. [2]Bring in the animals, too—a pair of each, except those kinds I have chosen for eating and for sacrifice: take seven pairs of each of them, [3]and seven pairs of every kind of bird. Thus there will be every kind of life reproducing again after the flood has ended. [4]One week from today I will begin forty days and nights of rain; and all the animals and birds and reptiles I have made will die."

[5]So Noah did everything the Lord commanded him. [6]He was 600 years old when the flood came. [7]He boarded the boat with his wife and sons and their wives, to escape the flood. [8,9]With him were all the various kinds of animals—those for eating and sacrifice, and those that were not, and the birds and reptiles. They came into the boat in pairs, male and female, just as God commanded Noah.

God Sends a Great Flood
[10-12]One week later, when Noah was 600 years, two months, and seventeen days old, the rain came down in mighty torrents from the sky, and the subterranean waters burst forth upon the earth for forty days and nights. [13]But Noah had gone into the boat that very day with his wife and his sons, Shem, Ham, and Japheth,

and their wives. [14,15]With them in the boat were pairs of every kind of animal—domestic and wild—and reptiles and birds of every sort. [16]Two by two they came, male and female, just as God had commanded. Then the Lord God closed the door and shut them in.

[17]For forty days the roaring floods prevailed, covering the ground and lifting the boat high above the earth. [18]As the water rose higher and higher above the ground, the boat floated safely upon it; [19]until finally the water covered all the high mountains under the whole heaven, [20]standing twenty-two feet and more above the highest peaks. [21]And all living things upon the earth perished—birds, domestic and wild animals, and reptiles and all mankind— [22]everything that breathed and lived upon dry land. [23]All existence on the earth was blotted out—man and animals alike, and reptiles and birds. God destroyed them all, leaving only Noah alive, and those with him in the boat. [24]And the water covered the earth 150 days.

CHAPTER 8
God didn't forget about Noah and all the animals in the boat! He sent a wind to blow across the waters, and the floods began to disappear, [2]for the subterranean water sources ceased their gushing, and the torrential rains subsided. [3,4]So the flood gradually receded until, 150 days after it began, the boat came to rest upon the mountains of Ararat. [5]Three months later, as the waters continued to go down, other mountain peaks appeared.

[6]After another forty days, Noah opened a porthole [7]and released a raven that flew back and forth until the earth was dry. [8]Meanwhile he sent out a dove to see if it could find dry ground, [9]but the dove found no place to light, and returned to Noah, for the water was still too high. So Noah held out his hand and drew the dove back into the boat.

6:22 One has to wonder whether God's instructions made any sense to Noah. God told him to build a gigantic boat far from the nearest body of navigable water. But here we see that Noah was obedient even though God's instructions were hard to understand. This is one of the secrets of success in any recovery program. We may not understand how everything works, but we do what God tells us is necessary for our recovery. When we step out in faith as Noah did, God will give us the success we seek.

8:1 Noah had listened to God and obeyed all his requests. But now the ark was floating over the earth on the flood waters—not an ideal situation to be in. But God didn't forget about Noah. It is comforting to know that when we obey God, he will not forget us. He will stand by us until his plans for us are complete.

9:1-17 Noah and his family were the only people left after the Flood. The comforts of civilization had been washed away. They had to start all over again. God gave Noah his special blessing and instituted a program that, if followed, would result in a healthy society. God has given us his Word, which contains the ultimate blueprint for healthy living. And just as God gave the human race a new start with Noah, he can give each of us a new start, too.

NOAH & SONS

Parents often wonder if they can have a positive effect on their children in our corrupt world. Noah leaves us with a good model of what a godly parent should be like. Noah was the only righteous man left in a generation of corrupt individuals. He led his family by example in a world that looked upon Noah as being "out of touch." Society mocked him for his belief in and obedience to God.

The principles of obedience to God, consistency, and patience were taught to Noah's sons and their wives. When judgment came upon the world, Noah, his wife, his sons, and their wives were spared. Later in life, after the Flood, the Bible tells us that Noah became drunk on the wine of his vineyard. Two of his sons (Shem and Japheth) responded to the situation in a godly manner while one (Ham) did not. Noah's drunkenness and Ham's subsequent indiscretion resulted in the suffering of some of Ham's descendants.

As we look at Noah's life, we are reminded that our children learn from our example. They often receive great blessings from the good things we do, but also suffer from our mistakes. All of us, like Noah, have made mistakes. But those mistakes can become insignificant through our repentance and obedience to God's Word. We must remember that children become like the adults who surround them.

STRENGTHS AND ACCOMPLISHMENTS:
- Noah was the only follower of God left in his generation.
- Noah was the second father of the human race.
- Noah taught his sons patience, consistency, and obedience to God.

WEAKNESSES AND MISTAKES:
- Noah embarrassed himself by getting drunk in front of his sons.
- Ham acted in an ungodly manner resulting in a curse upon some of his descendants.

LESSONS FROM THEIR LIVES:
- God is faithful to those who trust and obey him.
- Obedience to God is a lifelong commitment.
- Good parents teach their children by example.

KEY VERSE:
"And Noah did everything as God commanded him" (Genesis 6:22).

The story of Noah and his sons is told in Genesis 5:29–10:32. Noah is referred to in 1 Chronicles 1:4; Isaiah 54:9; Ezekiel 14:14, 20; Matthew 24:37-38; Luke 3:36; 17:26-27; Hebrews 11:7; 1 Peter 3:20; and 2 Peter 2:5.

---

[10]Seven days later Noah released the dove again, [11]and this time, toward evening, the bird returned to him with an olive leaf in her beak. So Noah knew that the water was almost gone. [12]A week later he released the dove again, and this time she didn't come back.
[13]Twenty-nine days after that, Noah opened the door to look, and the water was gone. [14]Eight more weeks went by. Then at last the earth was dry. [15,16]Then God told Noah, "You may all go out. [17]Release all the animals, birds, and reptiles, so that they will breed abundantly and reproduce in great numbers." [18,19]So the boat was soon empty. Noah, his wife, and his sons and their wives all disembarked, along with all the animals, reptiles, and birds—all left the ark in pairs and groups.
[20]Then Noah built an altar and sacrificed on it some of the animals and birds God had designated for that purpose. [21]And Jehovah was pleased with the sacrifice and said to himself, "I will never do it again—I will never again curse the earth, destroying all living things, even though man's bent is always toward evil from his earliest youth, and even though he does such wicked things. [22]As long as the earth remains, there will be springtime and harvest, cold and heat, winter and summer, day and night."

CHAPTER 9

God blessed Noah and his sons and told them to have many children and to repopulate the earth.

[2,3]"All wild animals and birds and fish will be afraid of you," God told him; "for I have placed them in your power, and they are yours to use for food, in addition to grain and vegetables. [4]But never eat animals unless their life-blood has been drained off. [5,6]And murder is forbidden. Man-killing animals must die, and any man who murders shall be killed; for to kill a man is to kill one made like God. [7]Yes, have many children and repopulate the earth and subdue it."

[8]Then God told Noah and his sons, [9-11]"I solemnly promise you and your children and

the animals you brought with you—all these birds and cattle and wild animals—that I will never again send another flood to destroy the earth. [12]And I seal this promise with this sign: [13]I have placed my rainbow in the clouds as a sign of my promise until the end of time, to you and to all the earth. [14]When I send clouds over the earth, the rainbow will be seen in the clouds, [15]and I will remember my promise to you and to every being, that never again will the floods come and destroy all life. [16,17]For I will see the rainbow in the cloud and remember my eternal promise to every living being on the earth."

Noah's Family

[18]The names of Noah's three sons were Shem, Ham, and Japheth. (Ham is the ancestor of the Canaanites.) [19]From these three sons of Noah came all the nations of the earth.

[20,21]Noah became a farmer and planted a vineyard, and he made wine. One day as he was drunk and lay naked in his tent, [22]Ham, the father of Canaan, saw his father's nakedness and went outside and told his two brothers.

[23]Then Shem and Japheth took a robe and held it over their shoulders and, walking backwards into the tent, let it fall across their father to cover his nakedness as they looked the other way. [24,25]When Noah awoke from his drunken stupor, and learned what had happened and what Ham, his younger son, had done, he cursed Ham's descendants:

"A curse upon the Canaanites," he swore.
"May they be the lowest of slaves
To the descendants of Shem and Japheth."

[26,27]Then he said,

"God bless Shem,
And may Canaan be his slave.
God bless Japheth,
And let him share the prosperity of Shem,
And let Canaan be his slave."

[28]Noah lived another 350 years after the flood [29]and was 950 years old at his death.

CHAPTER 10

These are the families of Shem, Ham, and Japheth, who were the three sons of Noah; for sons were born to them after the flood.

[2]The sons of Japheth were: Gomer, Magog, Madai, Javan, Tubal, Meshech, Tiras.

[3]The sons of Gomer: Ashkenaz, Riphath, Togarmah.

[4]The sons of Javan: Elishah, Tarshish, Kittim, Dodanim.

[5]Their descendants became the maritime nations in various lands, each with a separate language.

[6]The sons of Ham were: Cush, Mizraim, Put, Canaan.

[7]The sons of Cush were: Seba, Havilah, Sabtah, Raamah, Sabteca.

The sons of Raamah were: Sheba, Dedan.

[8]One of the descendants of Cush was Nimrod, who became the first of the kings.[9]He was a mighty hunter, blessed of God, and his name became proverbial. People would speak of someone as being "like Nimrod—a mighty hunter, blessed of God." [10]The heart of his empire included Babel, Erech, Accad, and Calneh in the land of Shinar. [11,12]From there he extended his reign to Assyria. He built Nineveh, Rehoboth-Ir, Calah, and Resen (which is located between Nineveh and Calah), the main city of the empire.

[13,14]Mizraim was the ancestor of the people inhabiting these areas: Ludim, Anamim, Lehabim, Naphtuhim, Pathrusim, Casluhim (from whom came the Philistines), and Caphtorim.

[15-19]Canaan's oldest son was Sidon, and he was also the father of Heth; from Canaan descended these nations: Jebusites, Amorites, Girgashites, Hivites, Arkites, Sinites, Arvadites, Zemarites, Hamathites. Eventually the descendants of Canaan spread from Sidon all the way to Gerar, in the Gaza strip; and to Sodom, Gomorrah, Admah, and Zeboiim, near Lasha.

[20]These, then, were the descendants of Ham, spread abroad in many lands and nations, with many languages.

[21]Eber descended from Shem, the oldest brother of Japheth. [22]Here is a list of Shem's other descendants: Elam, Asshur, Arpachshad, Lud, Aram.

9:20-21 With all the talk of Noah's righteousness and his fellowship with God, it is surprising to read that, by his choice, he fell prey to the excesses of alcohol. The account of Noah's drunkenness and shame comes as a shock to the reader, but it is a reminder that even in ideal conditions it is easy for us to slip and fall. We can never relax and feel as if we have it made, for that is when we become most vulnerable to failure.

10:1-32 This chapter is often called the Table of Nations. It is refreshing to realize that the God we worship is not a local deity. He is sovereign over all ethnic and language groups, nations, and political entities. The God who holds kings and empires in his hands surely has the power to hold us, too.

ABRAHAM & SARAH

Many give lip service to walking by faith; Abraham and Sarah modeled it. They were imperfect but willing instruments used by God to implement his perfect plan.

Abram, with Sarai, departed by faith from a pagan world for a new life of God's choosing. God promised a land and a nation of descendants, including One through whom all the peoples of the world would be blessed. The covenant defied human logic: Abram was seventy-five; Sarai was ten years younger and infertile. Their hopes of children had long vanished. Yet Abram believed God's promises.

During their pilgrimage, the pair often strayed from God's will. They succumbed to fear and dishonesty in dealings with Pharaoh and Abimelech. Difficulty in persevering led them to second-guess God. Abram's resulting union with Hagar resulted in domestic strife. Jealousy naturally erupted, and family relationships became strained. Abram behaved irresponsibly and Sarai acted with deliberate cruelty. Years later a wiser Abraham would listen to God's instructions for handling the handmaid and her son.

Abram's and Sarai's failures neither diminished God's love for them nor altered his commitment to his promises. Through turmoil and temptation, the couple's mutual affection and respect survived. Eventually God changed their names. Sarah's faith grew, and a quarter-century after God's promises were first given, she bore a son. They named him Isaac. The delayed gratification must have been sweet! Sarah enjoyed Isaac for many years, and after her death she was tenderly mourned by both husband and son.

Worship and obedience were such a part of Abraham's life that when God tested Abraham's faith, he willingly surrendered his son, Isaac, for a sacrifice. Then, God provided a lamb as a burnt offering to take Isaac's place on the altar. God's provision in Abraham's life can bring hope to us even today.

STRENGTHS AND ACCOMPLISHMENTS:
- They voluntarily left comfortable, familiar surroundings to pursue God's will.
- Both are heralded in Scripture as examples of faithful obedience.
- Abraham's physical descendants include the Jewish nation, from which came Jesus the Messiah.
- Abraham's spiritual descendants include all who have trusted Jesus for salvation.

WEAKNESSES AND MISTAKES:
- They at times presumed to know God's plans before he revealed them and attempted foolishly to assist him.
- When victimized by fear, Abraham was not above protecting himself at the expense of his wife's safety and integrity.
- Both acted intolerably toward Hagar and her son.

LESSONS FROM THEIR LIVES:
- A fresh start is possible at any stage of life.
- The fulfillment of God's promises does not depend upon our performance, but upon his grace.
- It is dangerous to move ahead without first seeking God's direction.

KEY VERSE:
"Then God did as he had promised, and Sarah became pregnant and gave Abraham a baby son in his old age, at the time God had said" (Genesis 21:1-2).

The story of Abraham and Sarah is found in Genesis 11–25. Among the many other references to Abraham are Romans 4:1-24; 9:7-9; Galatians 3:6-9, 14, 18; James 2:21-23; Hebrews 6:13-15; 7:1-2, 4-6; 11:8-12, 17-19. Sarah is mentioned in Romans 4:19; 9:9; Hebrews 11:11; and 1 Peter 3:6.

---

²³Aram's sons were: Uz, Hul, Gether, Mash. ²⁴Arpachshad's son was Shelah, and Shelah's son was Eber.

²⁵Two sons were born to Eber: Peleg (meaning "Division," for during his lifetime the people of the world were separated and dispersed), and Joktan (Peleg's brother).

²⁶⁻³⁰Joktan was the father of Almodad, Sheleph, Hazarmaveth, Jerah, Hadoram, Uzal, Diklah, Obal, Abima-el, Sheba, Ophir, Havilah, Jobab.

These descendants of Joktan lived all the way from Mesha to the eastern hills of Sephar.

³¹These, then, were the descendants of Shem, classified according to their political groupings, languages, and geographical locations.

³²All of the men listed above descended from Noah, through many generations, living in the various nations that developed after the flood.

CHAPTER 11
The Tower of Babel
At that time all mankind spoke a single language. ²As the population grew and spread eastward, a plain was discovered in the land

of Babylon and was soon thickly populated. 3,4The people who lived there began to talk about building a great city, with a temple-tower reaching to the skies—a proud, eternal monument to themselves.

"This will weld us together," they said, "and keep us from scattering all over the world." So they made great piles of hardburned brick, and collected bitumen to use as mortar.

5But when God came down to see the city and the tower mankind was making, 6he said, "Look! If they are able to accomplish all this when they have just *begun* to exploit their linguistic and political unity, just think of what they will do later! Nothing will be unattainable for them! 7Come, let us go down and give them different languages, so that they won't understand each other's words!"

8So, in that way, God scattered them all over the earth; and that ended the building of the city. 9That is why the city was called Babel (meaning "confusion"), because it was there that Jehovah confused them by giving them many languages, thus widely scattering them across the face of the earth.

Shem's Family

10,11Shem's line of descendants included Arpachshad, born two years after the flood when Shem was 100 years old; after that he lived another 500 years and had many sons and daughters.

12,13When Arpachshad was thirty-five years old, his son Shelah was born, and after that he lived another 403 years and had many sons and daughters.

14,15Shelah was thirty years old when his son Eber was born, living 403 years after that, and had many sons and daughters.

16,17Eber was thirty-four years old when his son Peleg was born. He lived another 430 years afterwards and had many sons and daughters.

18,19Peleg was thirty years old when his son Reu was born. He lived another 209 years afterwards and had many sons and daughters.

20,21Reu was thirty-two years old when Serug was born. He lived 207 years after that, with many sons and daughters.

22,23Serug was thirty years old when his son Nahor was born. He lived 200 years afterwards, with many sons and daughters.

24,25Nahor was twenty-nine years old at the birth of his son Terah. He lived 119 years afterwards and had sons and daughters.

26By the time Terah was seventy years old, he had three sons, Abram, Nahor, and Haran.

27And Haran had a son named Lot. 28But Haran died young, in the land where he was born (in Ur of the Chaldeans), and was survived by his father.

29Meanwhile, Abram married his half sister Sarai, while his brother Nahor married their orphaned niece, Milcah, who was the daughter of their brother Haran; and she had a sister named Iscah. 30But Sarai was barren; she had no children. 31Then Terah took his son Abram, his grandson Lot (his son Haran's child), and his daughter-in-law Sarai, and left Ur of the Chaldeans to go to the land of Canaan; but they stopped instead at the city of Haran and settled there. 32And there Terah died at the age of 205.

11:3-4 Whatever else the Tower of Babel might have represented, it was a mighty monument to human pride. It was a symbol of man's rebellion against the revealed will of God. This type of pride is always destructive to human community and to the process of recovery.

11:5-9 The Tower of Babel incident records the progression of broken communication that began back in the Garden of Eden. After sin entered the world, Adam and Eve began to hide the truth. They tried to blame each other and God for their mistakes, resulting in separation from God and barriers between that first couple. The sinful pride of the people of Babel caused another great rift in human communication. Numerous languages now divided them into various groups making their cooperation difficult, if not impossible. But the story doesn't end there. God is in the business of restoring broken communication. He chose the nation of Israel and spoke to them, giving them his laws. His Son was born through this nation, so he could speak to us and walk among us. And when the Holy Spirit came, the diversity of language was no longer a barrier to communication (Acts 2:5-12). God's program is designed to enhance our communication with him and the people around us.

12:1 A relationship with God is a two-way street. He is there to help us, but he also expects us to follow his plan. When God called Abram to leave his country and his people and to go to a land that God would show him, God promised to guide him. But Abram had to step out in faith. God has promised to be with us as we seek his help in recovery, but he may also ask something of us. As with Abraham, God may call us away from the familiar world that drags us down. And if we want to progress, we will need to follow his plan.

LOT & FAMILY

Many people in this world live for wealth, comfort, and the easy life. And they want to get it as quickly as possible! To make this happen, they often sacrifice the really important things in life. This was true in the life of Abraham's nephew Lot. Looking for the easy road to wealth and comfort, he made decisions that ended up destroying everything he had lived for.

Lot always thought of himself first. He demonstrated this when he chose the rich pastureland of the valleys, leaving Abraham with the rugged hill country. Embracing the easy comforts of the valley's cities and the physical prosperity they offered, he grew blind to the legacy he was leaving his descendants. When the men of Sodom demanded that Lot send his angelic guests out to take part in their sexual practices, Lot offered his daughters as an alternative. His desire to be accepted by the sinful people of his adopted homeland led him to fail to treat his daughters with the respect and protection they deserved.

The result of Lot's selfishness and greed was the loss of his fortune and the ruin of his family. He sacrificed all he had worked for and his family to the gods of comfort and wealth. He witnessed his wife's death as a result of her disobedience to God—something he had modeled for her. His daughters followed Lot's example, too. They used the quickest and easiest means available to overcome their lonely and childless state—drunkenness, seduction, and incest.

Our society places great value on wealth, comfort, and success, calling us all to join the mad rush to get them. This focus is so pervasive that it may be hard for us to see it as being bad. But though living for wealth may not seem such a terrible sin, its destructive effects upon people in our world are widespread. We must learn to put God first. If we put wealth first, we will lose all the really important things in life—our family and our relationship with God.

STRENGTHS AND ACCOMPLISHMENTS:
- Lot was successful at generating wealth.
- The apostle Peter referred to him as a just and righteous man.

WEAKNESSES AND MISTAKES:
- Lot often chose the easiest course of action, and usually at the expense of doing what was right.
- When faced with making a decision, Lot thought of himself first.
- Lot's daughters used sinful means to meet their needs instead of seeking God's provision.

LESSONS FROM THEIR LIVES:
- If we live for comfort and wealth, they will come between us and our family.
- We need to take care of our responsibilities to God and people first if we want our life to be successful.
- Mistakes made by parents usually lead to mistakes made by their children.
- When we put wealth and comfort before obedience to God, the result will be destructive.

KEY VERSE:
"Come, let's fill him [Lot] with wine and then we will sleep with him, so that our clan will not come to an end" (Genesis 19:32).

The story of Lot and his family is told in Genesis 13 and 19. Lot is also mentioned in Deuteronomy 2:9; Luke 17:28-32; and 2 Peter 2:7-8.

CHAPTER 12
Abram Begins a New Life
God had told Abram, "Leave your own country behind you, and your own people, and go to the land I will guide you to. 2If you do, I will cause you to become the father of a great nation; I will bless you and make your name famous, and you will be a blessing to many others. 3I will bless those who bless you and curse those who curse you; and the entire world will be blessed because of you."

4So Abram departed as the Lord had instructed him, and Lot went too; Abram was seventy-five years old at that time. 5He took his wife Sarai, his nephew Lot, and all his wealth—the cattle and slaves he had gotten in Haran—and finally arrived in Canaan. 6Traveling through Canaan, they came to a place near Shechem, and set up camp beside the oak at Moreh. (This area was inhabited by Canaanites at that time.)

7Then Jehovah appeared to Abram and said, "I am going to give this land to your descendants." And Abram built an altar there to commemorate Jehovah's visit. 8Afterwards Abram left that place and traveled southward to the hilly country between Bethel on the west and Ai on the east. There he made camp, and made an altar to the Lord and prayed to him. ⁹Thus he continued slowly southward to the Negeb, pausing frequently.

Abram Deceives Pharaoh

¹⁰There was at that time a terrible famine in the land: and so Abram went on down to Egypt to live. ¹¹⁻¹³But as he was approaching the borders of Egypt, he asked Sarai his wife to tell everyone that she was his sister! "You are very beautiful," he told her, "and when the Egyptians see you they will say, 'This is his wife. Let's kill him and then we can have her!' But if you say you are my sister, then the Egyptians will treat me well because of you, and spare my life!" ¹⁴And sure enough, when they arrived in Egypt everyone spoke of her beauty. ¹⁵When the palace aides saw her, they praised her to their king, the Pharaoh, and she was taken into his harem. ¹⁶Then Pharaoh gave Abram many gifts because of her— sheep, oxen, donkeys, men and women slaves, and camels.

¹⁷But the Lord sent a terrible plague upon Pharaoh's household on account of her being there. ¹⁸Then Pharaoh called Abram before him and accused him sharply. "What is this you have done to me?" he demanded. "Why didn't you tell me she was your wife? ¹⁹Why were you willing to let me marry her, saying she was your sister? Here, take her and be gone!" ²⁰And Pharaoh sent them out of the country under armed escort—Abram, his wife, and all his household and possessions.

CHAPTER 13
Lot Leaves Abram

So they left Egypt and traveled north into the Negeb—Abram with his wife, and Lot, and all that they owned, for Abram was very rich in livestock, silver, and gold. ³,⁴Then they continued northward toward Bethel where he had camped before, between Bethel and Ai— to the place where he had built the altar. And there he again worshiped the Lord.

⁵Lot too was very wealthy, with sheep and cattle and many servants. ⁶But the land could not support both Abram and Lot with all their flocks and herds. There were too many animals for the available pasture. ⁷So fights broke out between the herdsmen of Abram and Lot, despite the danger they all faced from the tribes of Canaanites and Perizzites present in the land. ⁸Then Abram talked it over with Lot. "This fighting between our men has got to stop," he said. "We can't afford to let a rift develop between our clans. Close relatives such as we are must present a united front! ⁹I'll tell you what we'll do. Take your choice of any section of the land you want, and we will separate. If you want that part over there to the east, then I'll stay here in the western section. Or, if you want the west, then I'll go over there to the east."

¹⁰Lot took a long look at the fertile plains of the Jordan River, well watered everywhere (this was before Jehovah destroyed Sodom and Gomorrah); the whole section was like the Garden of Eden, or like the beautiful countryside around Zoar in Egypt. ¹¹So that is what Lot chose—the Jordan valley to the east of them. He went there with his flocks and servants, and thus he and Abram parted company. ¹²For Abram stayed in the land of Canaan, while Lot lived among the cities of the plain, settling at a place near the city of Sodom. ¹³The men of this area were unusually wicked, and sinned greatly against Jehovah.

¹⁴After Lot was gone, the Lord said to Abram, "Look as far as you can see in every

---

12:11-20 As Abram and Sarai approached Egypt, Abram began to fear that the Egyptians would kill him to take his beautiful wife. So Abram and Sarai spun a lie to "protect" their relationship. They spread a story that they were brother and sister. This was a half-truth—they were half siblings. But it should be recognized that a half-truth is a whole lie. And like most lies, this one backfired, almost destroying Abram and Sarai's marriage. Total honesty is an essential part of our recovery. We need to be careful to avoid doing what Abram and Sarai did, even though they did it with the best of intentions. Dishonesty never pays—never try to rationalize it.

13:5-11 A conflict developed between the families of Abram and Lot over pastureland for their flocks. To strengthen the strained family relationship, Abram offered Lot first choice of the land. Abram realized that people were more important than possessions, so he sacrificed his right to the best land to maintain harmony between their families. In recovery, we need to learn this important lesson: our relationships are more important than the things we own.

13:11-13 One bad choice often leads to another. The choices Lot made here and in the following chapters led him toward his later fall. Here, he selfishly chose the best land and the easy life-style that would accompany it. In 13:12-13, he chose to move closer to the wicked city of Sodom. In 19:1-18, he chose to become an important man in a wicked place. In 19:30-38, his fall reached its final depths as he had incestuous relations with his daughters. We need to think ahead, reflecting upon the probable consequences of our present decisions.

direction, ¹⁵for I am going to give it all to you and your descendants. ¹⁶And I am going to give you so many descendants that, like dust, they can't be counted! ¹⁷Hike in all directions and explore the new possessions I am giving you." ¹⁸Then Abram moved his tent to the oaks of Mamre, near Hebron, and built an altar to Jehovah there.

CHAPTER 14
Abram Rescues Lot

Now war filled the land—Amraphel, king of Shinar, Arioch, king of Ellasar, Ched-or-laomer, king of Elam, and Tidal, king of Goiim ²fought against: Bera, king of Sodom, Birsha, king of Gomorrah, Shinab, king of Admah, Shemeber, king of Zeboiim, and the king of Bela (later called Zoar).

³These kings (of Sodom, Gomorrah, Admah, Zeboiim, and Bela) mobilized their armies in Siddim Valley (that is, the valley of the Dead Sea). ⁴For twelve years they had all been subject to King Ched-or-laomer, but now in the thirteenth year, they rebelled.

⁵,⁶One year later, Ched-or-laomer and his allies arrived and the slaughter began. For they were victorious over the following tribes at the places indicated: the Rephaim in Ashteroth-karnaim; the Zuzim in Ham; the Emim in the plain of Kiriathaim; the Horites in Mount Seir, as far as El-paran at the edge of the desert.

⁷Then they swung around to Enmishpat (later called Kadesh) and destroyed the Amalekites, and also the Amorites living in Hazazan-tamar.

⁸,⁹But now the other army, that of the kings of Sodom, Gomorrah, Admah, Zeboiim, and Bela (Zoar), unsuccessfully attacked Ched-or-laomer and his allies as they were in the Dead Sea Valley (four kings against five). ¹⁰As it happened, the valley was full of asphalt pits. And as the army of the kings of Sodom and Gomorrah fled, some slipped into the pits, and the remainder fled to the mountains. ¹¹Then the victors plundered Sodom and Gomorrah and carried off all their wealth and food, and went on their homeward way, ¹²taking with them Lot—Abram's nephew who lived in Sodom—and all he owned. ¹³One of the men who escaped came and told Abram the Hebrew, who was camping among the oaks belonging to Mamre the Amorite (brother of Eshcol and Aner, Abram's allies).

¹⁴When Abram learned that Lot had been captured, he called together the men born into his household, 318 of them in all, and

▶ **The Twelve Step devotional reading plan begins here.**

No-Win Situations

BIBLE READING: Genesis 16:1-15
We admitted that we were powerless over our dependencies—that our life had become unmanageable.
Sometimes we are powerless because of our station in life. We may be in a situation where other people have power over us. We may feel that we are trapped by the demands of others, and that there's no way to please them all. It's a double bind: to please one is to disappoint another. Sometimes when we feel stuck and frustrated with our relationships, we look for a measure of control by escaping through our addictive behaviors.

Hagar is a picture of powerlessness. She had no rights. As a girl, she was a slave to Sarai and Abram. When they were upset because Sarai could not bear children, Hagar was given to Abram as a surrogate. When she did become pregnant, as they had wanted, Sarai was so jealous that she beat the girl and she ran away. All alone, out in the wilderness, she was met by an Angel who told her, "Return to your mistress and act as you should, for I will make you into a great nation. Yes, you are pregnant and your baby will be a son, and you are to name him Ishmael ('God hears'), because God has heard your woes" (Genesis 16:9-11).

When we are caught in no-win situations, it's tempting to run away through our addictive/compulsive escape hatches. At times like these God is there, and he is listening to our woes. We need to learn to express our pain to God instead of just trying to escape. He hears our cries and is willing to give us hope for the future. *Turn to page 283, Judges 16.*

chased after the retiring army as far as Dan.
[15]He divided his men and attacked during the
night from several directions, and pursued
the fleeing army to Hobah, north of Damas-
cus, [16]and recovered everything—the loot that
had been taken, his relative Lot, and all of
Lot's possessions, including the women and
other captives.

[17]As Abram returned from his strike against
Ched-or-laomer and the other kings at the
Valley of Shaveh (later called King's Valley),
the king of Sodom came out to meet him,
[18]and Melchizedek, the king of Salem (Jerusa-
lem), who was a priest of the God of Highest
Heaven, brought him bread and wine.
[19,20]Then Melchizedek blessed Abram with this
blessing:

"The blessing of the supreme God, Creator
of heaven and earth, be upon you,
Abram; and blessed be God, who has
delivered your enemies over to you."

Then Abram gave Melchizedek a tenth of all
the loot.
[21]The king of Sodom told him, "Just give me
back my people who were captured; keep for
yourself the booty stolen from my city."
[22]But Abram replied, "I have solemnly
promised Jehovah, the supreme God, Creator
of heaven and earth, [23]that I will not take so
much as a single thread from you, lest you say,
'Abram is rich because of what I gave him!'
[24]All I'll accept is what these young men of
mine have eaten; but give a share of the loot
to Aner, Eshcol, and Mamre, my allies."

CHAPTER 15
God Gives Abram a Promise
Afterwards Jehovah spoke to Abram in a vision, and this is what he told him: "Don't be
fearful, Abram, for I will defend you. And I
will give you great blessings."

[2,3]But Abram replied, "O Lord Jehovah,
what good are all your blessings when I have
no son? For without a son, some other member of my household will inherit all my
wealth."

[4]Then Jehovah told him, "No, no one else
will be your heir, for you will have a son to
inherit everything you own."

[5]Then God brought Abram outside beneath
the nighttime sky and told him, "Look up
into the heavens and count the stars if you
can. Your descendants will be like that—too
many to count!" [6]And Abram believed God;
then God considered him righteous on account of his faith.

[7]And he told him, "I am Jehovah who
brought you out of the city of Ur of the
Chaldeans, to give you this land."

[8]But Abram replied, "O Lord Jehovah, how
can I be sure that you will give it to me?"
[9]Then Jehovah told him to take a three-year-
old heifer, a three-year-old female goat, a
three-year-old ram, a turtledove and a young
pigeon, [10]and to slay them and to cut them
apart down the middle, and to separate the
halves, but not to divide the birds. [11]And
when the vultures came down upon the carcasses, Abram shooed them away.
[12]That evening as the sun was going down,

14:14-16 A number of important character traits emerge as we examine Abram's prompt military action. He proved himself to be a man of courage, always ready to act when the situation demanded it. He was willing to give up certain luxuries in order to follow the program God had laid out for him. These are important characteristics for us to emulate as we continue in our recovery.
15:4-5 Because of the frustration of seventy-five childless years, God's promise of numerous children must have stretched Abram's faith to the very limit. God's plan for Abram seemed an impossibility—thousands of descendants from an old man and a barren woman. But God's promise did actually come about. God's plans for us may be beyond belief—even impossible. We may think we are beyond hope. But with God, nothing is impossible!
15:6 This is one of the most important verses in the Old Testament. Abram believed God, and God considered him righteous. In other words, it was Abram's faith, not his works, that made him righteous before God. For us to continue in recovery, we need to trust God more and trust our works less. We are powerless over the pressures of sin, but God will help us through the toughest temptations if we trust him. He will count us righteous because of our trust in him, not because we are perfect.
16:1-4 Since God's promise of a child had been given, about two years had passed without anything happening. Sometimes the hardest part of our recovery is the waiting. Here Abram and Sarai show us what not to do when things don't progress as quickly as we might hope. Rather than accepting God's timing, they took matters into their own hands. They assigned a servant girl, Hagar, to be a surrogate mother for Abram's son. This "solution" has been a source of conflict to this day. Abram's descendants through Hagar are the Arab nations whose conflict with the Jews keeps the Middle East in constant turmoil.

HAGAR & ISHMAEL

Hagar is often overshadowed by the two prominent people in her life—Abraham and Sarah. Her story is woven into the fabric of great events that make up Abraham's life. Yet God chose this "insignificant" woman to bear the son who was destined to be the father of the Arab nations.

When Hagar became pregnant, she gave in to her motherly pride and looked down on her mistress, Sarah, who had been unable to bear children. This prompted a great deal of strife in Abraham's family and much suffering for Hagar. The pain and alienation she suffered because of the baby could have put considerable strain on the mother-child relationship from the beginning. But Hagar showed no regrets about having her son. She joyfully received him and accepted him despite the complicated and emotionally charged circumstances surrounding his birth.

Hagar and her son, Ishmael, had much in common. They were both rejected by Abraham's household. Together they experienced the torture of the hot, barren desert after Sarah demanded that Abraham send them away. They became nameless outcasts, discarded by those who had once valued them. Under such circumstances, it must have been difficult to maintain a positive self-assessment.

Yet this mother and son persevered through these trials because they had faith in God, who had appeared to them in the wilderness. They knew that they were of great worth in his sight, and they rebuilt their identity upon his promises. To this day their story is used to illustrate God's deep concern for all who have been discarded and rejected. It also shows us that God's assessment of our life is far more important that what other people think.

STRENGTHS AND ACCOMPLISHMENTS:
- Hagar was willing to humbly return to Sarah even though she had been badly mistreated.
- Hagar stood by her son even though he was the source of many of her trials.

WEAKNESSES AND MISTAKES:
- When Hagar became pregnant, she pridefully looked down on Sarah, prompting much of the strife that followed.
- Hagar momentarily abandoned her son under a tree at the time of his greatest need.

LESSONS FROM THEIR LIVES:
- A loving mother/son relationship is a precious gift from God.
- God is deeply concerned about those who have been abused and rejected.
- God is able to restore a sense of self-worth even in the most trying times.

KEY VERSES:
"Return to your mistress and act as you should, for I will make you into a great nation. Yes, you are pregnant and your baby will be a son, and you are to name him Ishmael ('God hears'), because God has heard your woes" (Genesis 16:9-11).

The story of Hagar and Ishmael is told in Genesis 16–21. The apostle Paul briefly discusses them in Galatians 4:21-31.

---

a deep sleep fell upon Abram, and a vision of terrible foreboding, darkness, and horror.

[13]Then Jehovah told Abram, "Your descendants will be oppressed as slaves in a foreign land for 400 years. [14]But I will punish the nation that enslaves them, and at the end they will come away with great wealth. [15](But you will die in peace, at a ripe old age.) [16]After four generations they will return here to this land; for the wickedness of the Amorite nations living here now will not be ready for punishment until then."

[17]As the sun went down and it was dark, Abram saw a smoking firepot and a flaming torch that passed between the halves of the carcasses. [18]So that day Jehovah made this covenant with Abram: "I have given this land to your descendants from the Wadi-el-Arish to the Euphrates River. [19-21]And I give to them these nations: Kenites, Kenizzites, Kadmonites, Hittites, Perizzites, Rephaim, Amorites, Canaanites, Girgashites, Jebusites."

CHAPTER 16
Sarai Becomes Jealous of Hagar
But Sarai and Abram had no children. So Sarai took her maid, an Egyptian girl named Hagar, [2,3]and gave her to Abram to be his second wife.

"Since the Lord has given me no children," Sarai said, "you may sleep with my servant girl, and her children shall be mine."

And Abram agreed. (This took place ten years after Abram had first arrived in the land of Canaan.) [4]So he slept with Hagar, and she conceived; and when she realized she was pregnant, she became very proud and arrogant toward her mistress Sarai.

⁵Then Sarai said to Abram, "It's all your fault. For now this servant girl of mine despises me, though I myself gave her the privilege of being your wife. May the Lord judge you for doing this to me!"

⁶"You have my permission to punish the girl as you see fit," Abram replied. So Sarai beat her and she ran away.

⁷The Angel of the Lord found her beside a desert spring along the road to Shur.

⁸*The Angel:* "Hagar, Sarai's maid, where have you come from, and where are you going?"
Hagar: "I am running away from my mistress."
⁹⁻¹²*The Angel:* "Return to your mistress and act as you should, for I will make you into a great nation. Yes, you are pregnant and your baby will be a son, and you are to name him Ishmael ('God hears'), because God has heard your woes. This son of yours will be a wild one—free and untamed as a wild ass! He will be against everyone, and everyone will feel the same toward him. But he will live near the rest of his kin."

¹³Thereafter Hagar spoke of Jehovah—for it was he who appeared to her—as "the God who looked upon me," for she thought, "I saw God and lived to tell it."

¹⁴Later that well was named "The Well of the Living One Who Sees Me." It lies between Kadesh and Bered.

¹⁵So Hagar gave Abram a son, and Abram named him Ishmael. ¹⁶(Abram was eighty-six years old at this time.)

CHAPTER 17
God and Abram Make an Agreement

When Abram was ninety-nine years old, God appeared to him and told him, "I am the Almighty; obey me and live as you should. ²⁻⁴I will prepare a contract between us, guaranteeing to make you into a mighty nation. In fact you shall be the father of not only one nation, but a multitude of nations!" Abram fell face downward in the dust as God talked with him.

⁵"What's more," God told him, "I am changing your name. It is no longer 'Abram' ('Exalted Father'), but 'Abraham' ('Father of Nations')—for that is what you will be. I have declared it. ⁶I will give you millions of descendants who will form many nations! Kings shall be among your descendants! ⁷,⁸And I will continue this agreement between us generation after generation, forever, for it shall be between me and your children as well. It is a contract that I shall be your God and the God of your posterity. And I will give all this land of Canaan to you and them, forever. And I will be your God.

⁹,¹⁰"Your part of the contract," God told him, "is to obey its terms. You personally and all your posterity have this continual responsibility: that every male among you shall be circumcised; ¹¹the foreskin of his penis shall be cut off. This will be the proof that you and they accept this covenant. ¹²Every male shall be circumcised on the eighth day after birth. This applies to every foreign-born slave as well as to everyone born in your household. This is a permanent part of this contract, and it applies to all your posterity. ¹³All must be circumcised. Your bodies will thus be marked as participants in my everlasting covenant.

16:7-13 When Hagar was helpless to help herself, and when she recognized her powerlessness over her situation, the Angel of the Lord came and ministered to her. Until we recognize that our situation is unmanageable without outside help, God waits and does not enter the situation to help us. But when we are ready to admit our need and cry out, he is ready to step in.

17:5-6 Since Abram was childless, his name (meaning, "Exalted Father") must have been a source of embarrassment to him. Here it is changed to "Abraham," which means "Father of Nations." Abraham's name, in a real sense, became his promise from God. It would have been a continual reminder and source of hope that God would come through for him in the end.

17:9-10, 24-27 Most of our significant relationships are symbolized by an outward sign. For example, married people wear rings as a sign of their marriage commitment. Circumcision was a sign of the agreement or covenant between God and Abraham. It was a mark by which Abraham's descendants were set apart as God's special people. Inner changes need to be accompanied by outer signs; beliefs need to be proven by actions. In recovery, as changes begin to take place inside, we need to express these changes outwardly in our actions and life-style.

18:1-6 Hebrews 13:2 urges the practice of hospitality since some have "entertained angels without realizing it." Abraham's treatment of the three strangers here may have been the background for this verse in Hebrews. Surely this is an example to be followed. As we progress in recovery, one of our goals is to help others to discover the new way of life that we have found. What better way than to be hospitable toward others?

▶ **The Serenity Prayer devotional reading plan begins here.**

GOD grant me the serenity to accept the things I cannot change the courage to change the things I can and the wisdom to know the difference AMEN

We all face difficult situations that involve the people we love. In some of these situations the wise course of action may not be clear. We may feel a heavy burden to act, but have no idea what to do.

Abraham found himself in such a situation. The Lord had told Abraham that he intended to destroy the people of Sodom and Gomorrah for their wickedness. Since Abraham's nephew, Lot, lived among the people of these cities, Abraham was concerned for their welfare. So Abraham approached God and said, "'Will you kill good and bad alike? Suppose you find fifty godly people there within the city—will you destroy it, and not spare it for their sakes? That wouldn't be right! Surely you wouldn't do such a thing, to kill the godly with the wicked! . . . Should not the Judge of all the earth be fair?' And God replied, 'If I find fifty godly people there, I will spare the entire city for their sake'" (Genesis 18:23-26). The bargaining went on: Suppose there are only forty-five . . . forty . . . thirty . . . twenty . . . ten? And God said, "Then, for the sake of the ten, I won't destroy it" (18:32).

Abraham wasn't sure what he could do in the situation he faced; he wasn't even sure what was right in this situation. He talked it over with God, reasoning it out, trying to do whatever he could. When we don't know how much of a change we can or even should make, we can start by talking it over with God. Then we can try to do as much as we feel confident doing. *Turn to page 47, Genesis 37.*

---

[14] Anyone who refuses these terms shall be cut off from his people; for he has violated my contract."

[15] Then God added, "Regarding Sarai your wife—her name is no longer 'Sarai' but 'Sarah' ('Princess'). [16] And I will bless her and give you a son from her! Yes, I will bless her richly, and make her the mother of nations! Many kings shall be among her posterity."

[17] Then Abraham threw himself down in worship before the Lord, but inside he was laughing in disbelief! "Me, be a father?" he said in amusement. "Me—100 years old? And Sarah, to have a baby at 90?"

[18] And Abraham said to God, "Yes, do bless Ishmael!"

[19] "No," God replied, "that isn't what I said. *Sarah* shall bear you a son; and you are to name him Isaac ('Laughter'), and I will sign my covenant with him forever, and with his descendants. [20] As for Ishmael, all right, I will bless him also, just as you have asked me to. I will cause him to multiply and become a great nation. Twelve princes shall be among his posterity. [21] But my contract is with Isaac, who will be born to you and Sarah next year at about this time."

[22] That ended the conversation and God left. [23] Then, that very day, Abraham took Ishmael his son and every other male—born in his household or bought from outside—and cut off their foreskins, just as God had told him to. [24-27] Abraham was ninety-nine years old at that time, and Ishmael was thirteen. Both were circumcised the same day, along with all the other men and boys of the household, whether born there or bought as slaves.

CHAPTER 18
Angels Visit with Abraham
The Lord appeared again to Abraham while he was living in the oak grove at Mamre. This is the way it happened: One hot summer afternoon as he was sitting in the opening of

his tent, ²he suddenly noticed three men coming toward him. He sprang up and ran to meet them and welcomed them.

3,4"Sirs," he said, "please don't go any farther. Stop awhile and rest here in the shade of this tree while I get water to refresh your feet, ⁵and a bite to eat to strengthen you. Do stay awhile before continuing your journey."

"All right," they said, "do as you have said."

⁶Then Abraham ran back to the tent and said to Sarah, "Quick! Mix up some pancakes! Use your best flour, and make enough for the three of them!" ⁷Then he ran out to the herd and selected a fat calf and told a servant to hurry and butcher it. ⁸Soon, taking them cheese and milk and the roast veal, he set it before the men and stood beneath the trees beside them as they ate.

⁹"Where is Sarah, your wife?" they asked him.

"In the tent," Abraham replied.

¹⁰Then the Lord said, "Next year I will give you and Sarah a son!" (Sarah was listening from the tent door behind him.) ¹¹Now Abraham and Sarah were both very old, and Sarah was long since past the time when she could have a baby.

¹²So Sarah laughed silently. "A woman my age have a baby?" she scoffed to herself. "And with a husband as old as mine?"

¹³Then God said to Abraham, "Why did Sarah laugh? Why did she say 'Can an old woman like me have a baby?' ¹⁴Is anything too hard for God? Next year, just as I told you, I will certainly see to it that Sarah has a son."

¹⁵But Sarah denied it. "I didn't laugh," she lied, for she was afraid.

Abraham Intervenes for Sodom

¹⁶Then the men stood up from their meal and started on toward Sodom; and Abraham went with them part of the way.

¹⁷"Should I hide my plan from Abraham?" God asked. ¹⁸"For Abraham shall become a mighty nation, and he will be a source of blessing for all the nations of the earth. ¹⁹And

I have picked him out to have godly descendants and a godly household—men who are just and good—so that I can do for him all I have promised."

²⁰So the Lord told Abraham, "I have heard that the people of Sodom and Gomorrah are utterly evil, and that everything they do is wicked. ²¹I am going down to see whether these reports are true or not. Then I will know."

22,23So the other two went on toward Sodom, but the Lord remained with Abraham a while. Then Abraham approached him and said, "Will you kill good and bad alike? ²⁴Suppose you find fifty godly people there within the city—will you destroy it, and not spare it for their sakes? ²⁵That wouldn't be right! Surely you wouldn't do such a thing, to kill the godly with the wicked! Why, you would be treating godly and wicked exactly the same! Surely you wouldn't do that! Should not the Judge of all the earth be fair?"

²⁶And God replied, "If I find fifty godly people there, I will spare the entire city for their sake."

²⁷Then Abraham spoke again. "Since I have begun, let me go on and speak further to the Lord, though I am but dust and ashes. ²⁸Suppose there are only forty-five? Will you destroy the city for lack of five?"

And God said, "I will not destroy it if I find forty-five."

²⁹Then Abraham went further with his request. "Suppose there are only forty?"

And God replied, "I won't destroy it if there are forty."

³⁰"Please don't be angry," Abraham pleaded. "Let me speak: suppose only thirty are found there?"

And God replied, "I won't do it if there are thirty there."

³¹Then Abraham said, "Since I have dared to speak to God, let me continue—suppose there are only twenty?"

And God said, "Then I won't destroy it for the sake of the twenty."

³²Finally, Abraham said, "Oh, let not the

18:17-19 Many people wonder why God chose one man and his family out of all others. Was this fair? These verses show us that God had an important purpose for choosing this one family. God picked Abraham so he could teach his descendants God's ways, for through his ancestral line would come Jesus the Messiah, a source of blessing for all the nations of the earth. God never planned to bless only one family. God chose one family to bring blessings and a means of recovery to all of us.
18:22-32 Often, we are urged to pray for others who have problems and difficulties. In these verses, we hear Abraham as he entreats God on behalf of Lot and his family. He is deeply concerned for their welfare and intercedes for them as he speaks with God. This is similar to what we are asked to do in the twelfth step of our recovery. We are to reach out and help others who are in need. Prayer is a powerful means of doing this.

Lord be angry; I will speak but this once more! *Suppose only ten are found?"*

And God said, "Then, for the sake of the ten, I won't destroy it."

³³And the Lord went on his way when he had finished his conversation with Abraham. And Abraham returned to his tent.

CHAPTER 19
God Destroys Sodom

That evening the two angels came to the entrance of the city of Sodom, and Lot was sitting there as they arrived. When he saw them he stood up to meet them, and welcomed them.

²"Sirs," he said, "come to my home as my guests for the night; you can get up as early as you like and be on your way again."

"Oh, no thanks," they said, "we'll just stretch out here along the street."

³But he was very urgent, until at last they went home with him, and he set a great feast before them, complete with freshly baked unleavened bread. After the meal, ⁴as they were preparing to retire for the night, the men of the city—yes, Sodomites, young and old from all over the city—surrounded the house ⁵and shouted to Lot, "Bring out those men to us so we can rape them."

⁶Lot stepped outside to talk to them, shutting the door behind him. ⁷"Please, fellows," he begged, "don't do such a wicked thing. ⁸Look—I have two virgin daughters, and I'll surrender them to you to do with as you wish. But leave these men alone, for they are under my protection."

⁹"Stand back," they yelled. "Who do you think you are? We let this fellow settle among us and now he tries to tell us what to do! We'll deal with you far worse than with those other men." And they lunged at Lot and began breaking down the door.

¹⁰But the two men reached out and pulled Lot in and bolted the door ¹¹and temporarily blinded the men of Sodom so that they couldn't find the door.

¹²"What relatives do you have here in the city?" the men asked. "Get them out of this place—sons-in-law, sons, daughters, or anyone else. ¹³For we will destroy the city completely. The stench of the place has reached to heaven and God has sent us to destroy it."

¹⁴So Lot rushed out to tell his daughters' fiancés, "Quick, get out of the city, for the Lord is going to destroy it." But the young men looked at him as though he had lost his senses.

¹⁵At dawn the next morning the angels became urgent. "Hurry," they said to Lot, "take your wife and your two daughters who are here and get out while you can, or you will be caught in the destruction of the city."

¹⁶When Lot still hesitated, the angels seized his hand and the hands of his wife and two daughters and rushed them to safety, outside the city, for the Lord was merciful.

¹⁷"Flee for your lives," the angels told him. *"And don't look back.* Escape to the mountains. Don't stay down here on the plain or you will die."

¹⁸⁻²⁰"Oh no, sirs, please," Lot begged, "since you've been so kind to me and saved my life, and you've granted me such mercy, let me flee to that little village over there instead of into the mountains, for I fear disaster in the mountain. See, the village is close by and it is just a small one. Please, please, let me go there instead. Don't you see how small it is? And my life will be saved."

²¹"All right," the angel said, "I accept your proposition and won't destroy that little city. ²²But hurry! For I can do nothing until you are there." (From that time on that village was named Zoar, meaning "Little City.")

²³The sun was rising as Lot reached the village. ²⁴Then the Lord rained down fire and flaming tar from heaven upon Sodom and Gomorrah, ²⁵and utterly destroyed them, along with the other cities and villages of the plain, eliminating all life—people, plants, and animals alike. ²⁶But Lot's wife looked back as

---

19:16 Even after Lot became aware of the impending doom of Sodom, he and his family continued to linger there. The angels had to force them to leave. Sometimes, even when we know what course of action is required, we need a push to get us moving. Let us thank God for the "angels" he has provided to help us through times of crisis. Sometimes, as the twelfth step suggests, we may be needed to push others out of a situations that are dangerous for them.

19:17-26 As we seek recovery from our problems and dependencies there is no looking back, no lingering. Doing so will only result in our destruction. Lot's wife failed to follow the program that the angels had set out for her family. They were to run from Sodom, never to look back. Lot's wife did look back, and it spelled her destruction. As we leave the destructive situations in our life it will be tempting to look back. But this final episode in the life of Lot's wife demonstrates the fatal consequences. We need to run, without looking back.

she was following along behind him and became a pillar of salt.

[27]That morning Abraham was up early and hurried out to the place where he had stood before the Lord. [28]He looked out across the plain to Sodom and Gomorrah and saw columns of smoke and fumes, as from a furnace, rising from the cities there. [29]So God heeded Abraham's plea and kept Lot safe, removing him from the maelstrom of death that engulfed the cities.

The Sin of Lot's Daughters
[30]Afterwards Lot left Zoar, fearful of the people there, and went to live in a cave in the mountains with his two daughters. [31]One day the older girl said to her sister, "There isn't a man anywhere in this entire area that our father would let us marry. And our father will soon be too old for having children. [32]Come, let's fill him with wine and then we will sleep with him, so that our clan will not come to an end." [33]So they got him drunk that night, and the older girl went in and had sexual intercourse with her father; but he was unaware of her lying down or getting up again.

[34]The next morning she said to her younger sister, "I slept with my father last night. Let's fill him with wine again tonight, and you go in and lie with him, so that our family line will continue." [35]So they got him drunk again that night, and the younger girl went in and lay with him, and, as before, he didn't know that anyone was there. [36]And so it was that both girls became pregnant from their father. [37]The older girl's baby was named Moab; he became the ancestor of the nation of the Moabites. [38]The name of the younger girl's baby was Benammi; he became the ancestor of the nation of the Ammonites.

CHAPTER 20
Abraham Deceives Abimelech
Now Abraham moved south to the Negeb and settled between Kadesh and Shur. One day, when visiting the city of Gerar, [2]he declared that Sarah was his sister! Then King Abimelech sent for her, and had her brought to him at his palace.

[3]But that night God came to him in a dream and told him, "You are a dead man, for that woman you took is married."

[4]But Abimelech hadn't slept with her yet, so he said, "Lord, will you slay an innocent man? [5]He told me, 'She is my sister,' and she herself said, 'Yes, he is my brother.' I hadn't the slightest intention of doing anything wrong."

[6]"Yes, I know," the Lord replied. "That is why I held you back from sinning against me; that is why I didn't let you touch her. [7]Now restore her to her husband, and he will pray for you (for he is a prophet) and you shall live. But if you don't return her to him, you are doomed to death along with all your household."

[8]The king was up early the next morning, and hastily called a meeting of all the palace personnel and told them what had happened. And great fear swept through the crowd.

[9,10]Then the king called for Abraham. "What is this you've done to us?" he demanded. "What have I done that deserves treatment like this, to make me and my kingdom guilty of this great sin? Who would suspect that you would do a thing like this to me? Whatever made you think of this vile deed?"

[11,12]"Well," Abraham said, "I figured this to be a godless place. 'They will want my wife and will kill me to get her,' I thought. And besides, she *is* my sister—or at least a half sister (we both have the same father)—and I

19:30-38 The incest in Lot's family was a direct consequence of Lot's irresponsible decisions in the past. He had spent his years in a wicked city and had failed to find suitable husbands for his daughters. Their desire for children led to deceit and incest. But there is hope beyond the shocking details of this story. Even though Lot failed in so many ways, many centuries later the apostle Peter used him as a clear example of one whose righteousness came by grace through faith (2 Peter 2:7-8). Lot was an extremely flawed person; but God is a gracious God. There is hope available for each of us, no matter how sordid our past.

20:1-18 Why is it so difficult to learn life's most important lessons? To protect himself, Abraham lied, telling Abimelech that his wife, Sarah, was his sister. The sad truth is, Abraham had made this mistake before (12:10-20). He had fallen into a pattern of using lies and deceit to protect himself. But this practice only caused pain to everyone involved. It also displayed how weak Abraham's faith in God was when confronted with difficult situations. The truth is crucial to building healthy relationships. And if we stand by the truth, we can trust God to stand by us when things get tough.

21:1-2 God keeps his word. When we claim his promises, we know that our sovereign God is able to fulfill them. Under normal circumstances there was no way that Sarah could have become a mother. But God gave her a child anyway. Sometimes we may feel our recovery is just as impossible; but with God, it can be a reality. With him, anything is possible.

married her. [13]And when God sent me traveling far from my childhood home, I told her, 'Have the kindness to mention, wherever we come, that you are my sister.'"

[14]Then King Abimelech took sheep and oxen and servants—both men and women—and gave them to Abraham, and returned Sarah his wife to him.

[15]"Look my kingdom over, and choose the place where you want to live," the king told him. [16]Then he turned to Sarah. "Look," he said, "I am giving your 'brother' a thousand silver pieces as damages for what I did, to compensate for any embarrassment and to settle any claim against me regarding this matter. Now justice has been done."

[17]Then Abraham prayed, asking God to cure the king and queen and the other women of the household, so that they could have children; [18]for God had stricken all the women with barrenness to punish Abimelech for taking Abraham's wife.

CHAPTER 21
Isaac Is Born

Then God did as he had promised, and Sarah became pregnant and gave Abraham a baby son in his old age, at the time God had said; [3]and Abraham named him Isaac (meaning "Laughter!"). [4,5]Eight days after he was born, Abraham circumcised him, as God required. (Abraham was 100 years old at that time.)

[6]And Sarah declared, "God has brought me laughter! All who hear about this shall rejoice with me. [7]For who would have dreamed that I would ever have a baby? Yet I have given Abraham a child in his old age!"

[8]Time went by and the child grew and was weaned; and Abraham gave a party to celebrate the happy occasion. [9]But when Sarah noticed Ishmael—the son of Abraham and the Egyptian girl Hagar—teasing Isaac, [10]she turned upon Abraham and demanded, "Get rid of that slave girl and her son. He is not going to share your property with my son. I won't have it."

[11]This upset Abraham very much, for after all, Ishmael too was his son.

[12]But God told Abraham, "Don't be upset over the boy or your slave-girl wife; do as Sarah says, for Isaac is the son through whom my promise will be fulfilled. [13]And I will make a nation of the descendants of the slave-girl's son, too, because he also is yours."

[14]So Abraham got up early the next morning, prepared food for the journey, and strapped a canteen of water to Hagar's shoulders and sent

Faith

READ GENESIS 22:1-19

We demonstrate faith just by the fact that we are involved in a recovery program. If we didn't have faith in the promise of a better future for ourself and our family, we wouldn't put ourself through the hard work and pain involved in recovery. But as time passes, we may grow discouraged at the length of the process. We may have our spirits dampened by the ups and downs along the road, feeling our faith ebb more often than flow. Some people report instant release from their addictions, but for most of us it will take faith and patience to inherit the promise of a new life.

The writer of Hebrews wrote, "You will be anxious to follow the example of those who receive all that God has promised them because of their strong faith and patience. For instance, there was God's promise to Abraham: God took an oath in his own name, . . . that he would bless Abraham again and again, and give him a son and make him the father of a great nation of people. Then Abraham waited patiently until finally God gave him a son, Isaac, just as he had promised" (Hebrews 6:12-15). The entire story of Abraham's life can be found in Genesis 11–25.

The key point to consider here is that Abraham waited twenty-five years to see the promise fulfilled. As he waited, there were times when he showed impatience. At one point he took matters into his own hands, having a son by means of a surrogate wife. At times he probably wondered if he had ever really received the promise at all. He even laughed in disbelief when he was told the promise was soon to come about. But in the end he received the promise and "God blessed him in every way" (Genesis 24:1). Let's keep holding on! The fact that recovery usually takes time doesn't mean that our faith is in vain. *Turn to page 91, Exodus 20.*

her away with their son. She walked out into the wilderness of Beersheba, wandering aimlessly.

[15]When the water was gone she left the youth in the shade of a bush [16]and went off and sat down a hundred yards or so away. "I don't want to watch him die," she said, and burst into tears, sobbing wildly.

[17]Then God heard the boy crying, and the Angel of God called to Hagar from the sky, "Hagar, what's wrong? Don't be afraid! For God has heard the lad's cries as he is lying there. [18]Go and get him and comfort him, for I will make a great nation from his descendants."

[19]Then God opened her eyes and she saw a well; so she refilled the canteen and gave the lad a drink. [20,21]And God blessed the boy and he grew up in the wilderness of Paran, and became an expert archer. And his mother arranged a marriage for him with a girl from Egypt.

Abraham and Abimelech Agree

[22]About this time King Abimelech and Phicol, commander of his troops, came to Abraham and said to him, "It is evident that God helps you in everything you do; [23]swear to me by God's name that you won't defraud me or my son or my grandson, but that you will be on friendly terms with my country, as I have been toward you."

[24]Abraham replied, "All right, I swear to it!" [25]Then Abraham complained to the king about a well the king's servants had taken violently away from Abraham's servants.

[26]"This is the first I've heard of it," the king exclaimed, "and I have no idea who is responsible. Why didn't you tell me before?"

[27]Then Abraham gave sheep and oxen to the king, as sacrifices to seal their pact.

[28,29]But when he took seven ewe lambs and set them off by themselves, the king inquired, "Why are you doing that?"

[30]And Abraham replied, "They are my gift to you as a public confirmation that this well is mine."

[31]So from that time on the well was called Beer-sheba ("Well of the Oath"), because that was the place where they made their covenant. [32]Then King Abimelech and Phicol, commander of his army, returned home again. [33]And Abraham planted a tamarisk tree beside the well and prayed there to the Lord, calling upon the Eternal God. [34]And Abraham lived in the Philistine country for a long time.

CHAPTER 22
Abraham Offers His Only Son

Later on, God tested Abraham's [faith and obedience].

"Abraham!" God called.

"Yes, Lord?" he replied.

[2]"Take with you your only son—yes, Isaac whom you love so much—and go to the land of Moriah and sacrifice him there as a burnt offering upon one of the mountains which I'll point out to you!"

[3]The next morning Abraham got up early, chopped wood for a fire upon the altar, saddled his donkey, and took with him his son Isaac and two young men who were his servants, and started off to the place where God had told him to go. [4]On the third day of the journey Abraham saw the place in the distance.

[5]"Stay here with the donkey," Abraham told the young men, "and the lad and I will travel yonder and worship, and then come right back."

[6]Abraham placed the wood for the burnt

22:1-2 God's request that Abraham sacrifice his son was a great test of faith, perhaps the greatest such test in history. Abraham's lifelong dreams were being realized in his beloved son Isaac. Wasn't God's promise of numerous descendants to be fulfilled through this child? But Abraham believed that God had his best in mind—and Abraham was right! He believed that no matter what God required of him, his obedience to God's plan was most important. He trusted that God would still make his promises come true, even without Isaac. Our faith in God's program may be confronted by similar tests. Are we ready to follow through with obedience?

22:16-18 The love Abraham must have felt for this long-awaited son! How his heart must have ached at the thought of killing him! How could this have been right? At the end of the story we see that God spared Isaac by providing a ram as his substitute. God has provided a substitute for all of us—Jesus Christ. God did not spare himself the pain of seeing his Son suffer and die. He suffered so that we might be spared suffering and have a means for recovery from sin and its destructive effects.

23:1 In this chapter we see Abraham mourning for his precious wife, Sarah. His grief was genuine, and he wanted to make proper preparations for paying his last respects. Grief comes into each of our lives, and proper channels for its expression must be found. If we fail to grieve over our personal losses properly, it will be easy to fall into addictions and dependencies to try and hide the pain. If we express our pain constructively, it will be less likely to destroy us.

offering upon Isaac's shoulders, while he himself carried the knife and the flint for striking a fire. So the two of them went on together.

[7]"Father," Isaac asked, "we have the wood and the flint to make the fire, but where is the lamb for the sacrifice?"

[8]"God will see to it, my son," Abraham replied. And they went on.

[9]When they arrived at the place where God had told Abraham to go, he built an altar and placed the wood in order, ready for the fire, and then tied Isaac and laid him on the altar over the wood. [10]And Abraham took the knife and lifted it up to plunge it into his son, to slay him.

[11]At that moment the Angel of God shouted to him from heaven, "Abraham! Abraham!"

"Yes, Lord!" he answered.

[12]"Lay down the knife; don't hurt the lad in any way," the Angel said, "for I know that God is first in your life—you have not withheld even your beloved son from me."

[13]Then Abraham noticed a ram caught by its horns in a bush. So he took the ram and sacrificed it, instead of his son, as a burnt offering on the altar. [14]Abraham named the place "Jehovah provides"—and it still goes by that name to this day.

[15]Then the Angel of God called again to Abraham from heaven. [16]"I, the Lord, have sworn by myself that because you have obeyed me and have not withheld even your beloved son from me, [17]I will bless you with incredible blessings and multiply your descendants into countless thousands and millions, like the stars above you in the sky, and like the sands along the seashore. They will conquer their enemies, [18]and your offspring will be a blessing to all the nations of the earth—all because you have obeyed me."

[19]So they returned to his young men and traveled home again to Beer-sheba.

Nahor's Family

[20-23]After this, a message arrived that Milcah, the wife of Abraham's brother Nahor, had borne him eight sons. Their names were: Uz, the oldest, Buz, the next oldest, Kemuel (father of Aram), Chesed, Hazo, Pildash, Jidlaph, Bethuel (father of Rebekah).

[24]He also had four other children from his concubine, Reumah: Tebah, Gaham, Tahash, Maacah.

CHAPTER 23
Sarah Dies

When Sarah was 127 years old, she died in Hebron in the land of Canaan; there Abraham

Taking Time to Grieve

BIBLE READING: Genesis 23:1-4; 35:19-21

We were entirely ready for God to remove all these defects of character.

The pathway to recovery and finding new life also involves the death process. The different means we used to cope were "defective," but still, they did give us comfort or companionship. Giving them up is often like suffering the death of a loved one.

Abraham and his grandson, Jacob, both lost loved ones as they traveled to the Promised Land. "Sarah . . . died in Hebron in the land of Canaan; there Abraham mourned and wept for her. Then, standing beside her body, he said . . . 'Here I am, a visitor in a foreign land, with no place to bury my wife. Please sell me a piece of ground for this purpose.' . . . So Abraham buried Sarah there" (Genesis 23:1-4, 19). A generation later, Jacob was given a new name, Israel, and the promise of a great heritage in the Promised Land. On his way there, he, too, lost his beloved wife. She died while giving birth to their son Benjamin. "So Rachel died, and was buried near the road to Ephrath (also called Bethlehem). And Jacob set up a monument of stones upon her grave, and it is there to this day. Then Israel journeyed on" (Genesis 35:19-21).

As we journey on in our new life, we will necessarily lose some of our defective ways of coping. When this happens, we need to stop and take time to give our losses a proper burial. We need to put them away, cover the shame, and allow ourselves to grieve the loss of something very familiar to us. When the time of grieving is over, we, too, can journey on. *Turn to page 623, Psalm 51.*

mourned and wept for her. ³Then, standing beside her body, he said to the men of Heth:

⁴"Here I am, a visitor in a foreign land, with no place to bury my wife. Please sell me a piece of ground for this purpose."

⁵,⁶"Certainly," the men replied, "for you are an honored prince of God among us; it will be a privilege to have you choose the finest of our sepulchres, so that you can bury her there."

⁷Then Abraham bowed low before them and said, ⁸"Since this is your feeling in the matter, be so kind as to ask Ephron, Zohar's son, ⁹to sell me the cave of Mach-pelah, down at the end of his field. I will of course pay the full price for it, whatever is publicly agreed upon, and it will become a permanent cemetery for my family."

¹⁰Ephron was sitting there among the others, and now he spoke up, answering Abraham as the others listened, speaking publicly before all the citizens of the town: ¹¹"Sir," he said to Abraham, "please listen to me. I will give you the cave and the field without any charge. Here in the presence of my people, I give it to you free. Go and bury your dead."

¹²Abraham bowed again to the men of Heth, ¹³and replied to Ephron, as all listened: "No, let me buy it from you. Let me pay the full price of the field, and then I will bury my dead."

¹⁴,¹⁵"Well, the land is worth 400 pieces of silver," Ephron said, "but what is that between friends? Go ahead and bury your dead."

¹⁶So Abraham paid Ephron the price he had suggested—400 pieces of silver, as publicly agreed. ¹⁷,¹⁸This is the land he bought: Ephron's field at Mach-pelah, near Mamre, and the cave at the end of the field, and all the trees in the field. They became his permanent possession, by agreement in the presence of the men of Heth at the city gate. ¹⁹,²⁰So Abraham buried Sarah there, in the field and cave deeded to him by the men of Heth as a burial plot.

CHAPTER 24
Isaac Gets Married
Abraham was now a very old man, and God blessed him in every way. ²One day Abraham said to his household administrator, who was his oldest servant,

³"Swear by Jehovah, the God of heaven and earth, that you will not let my son marry one of these local girls, these Canaanites. ⁴Go instead to my homeland, to my relatives, and find a wife for him there."

⁵"But suppose I can't find a girl who will come so far from home?" the servant asked. "Then shall I take Isaac there, to live among your relatives?"

⁶"No!" Abraham warned. "Be careful that you don't do that under any circumstance. ⁷For the Lord God of heaven told me to leave that land and my people, and promised to give me and my children this land. He will send his angel on ahead of you, and he will see to it that you find a girl from there to be my son's wife. ⁸But if you don't succeed, then you are free from this oath; but under no circumstances are you to take my son there."

⁹So the servant vowed to follow Abraham's instructions.

¹⁰He took with him ten of Abraham's camels loaded with samples of the best of everything his master owned and journeyed to Iraq, to Nahor's village. ¹¹There he made the camels kneel down outside the town, beside a spring. It was evening, and the women of the village were coming to draw water.

¹²"O Jehovah, the God of my master," he prayed, "show kindness to my master Abraham and help me to accomplish the purpose of my journey. ¹³See, here I am, standing beside this spring, and the girls of the village are coming out to draw water. ¹⁴This is my request: When I ask one of them for a drink and she says, 'Yes, certainly, and I will water your camels too!'—let her be the one you have appointed as Isaac's wife. That is how I will know."

¹⁵,¹⁶As he was still speaking to the Lord about this, a beautiful young girl named Rebekah arrived with a water jug on her shoulder and filled it at the spring. (Her father was Bethuel the son of Nahor and his wife Milcah.) ¹⁷Running over to her, the servant asked her for a drink.

¹⁸"Certainly, sir," she said, and quickly lowered the jug for him to drink. ¹⁹Then she said, "I'll draw water for your camels, too, until they have enough!"

²⁰So she emptied the jug into the watering trough and ran down to the spring again and kept carrying water to the camels until they had enough. ²¹The servant said no more, but watched her carefully to see if she would finish the job, so that he would know whether she was the one. ²²Then at last, when the camels had finished drinking, he produced a quarter-ounce gold earring and two five-ounce gold bracelets for her wrists.

ISAAC & REBEKAH

Deception is extremely harmful in any relationship but even more so in the relationship of a husband and wife. Isaac and Rebekah started out with a marriage in which each loved and honored the other. However, as the marriage progressed, so did the deception on both sides. The end result was a family torn apart by strife.

As his father, Abraham, had done with Sarah, Isaac lied to Abimelech, claiming that Rebekah was not his wife. He did this to protect himself, fearing that Abimelech would kill him to take his wife. Deception based on the idea that "the end justifies the means" may at times seem a necessary evil within some families. But, in fact, it often starts a string of hurtful lies between marriage partners and other family members.

Isaac and Rebekah were blessed with twin sons, Esau and Jacob. Isaac liked Esau the best, while Rebekah preferred Jacob. This playing of favorites split the family in two and set the stage for further conflict and deception. When the time came for Isaac to give Esau his blessing, Jacob willingly took part in Rebekah's plan to deceive her husband. Deception had become a natural practice in this dysfunctional family.

This story of deception in a marriage is sad, but hardly uncommon. What started out as a loving marriage based on honesty and a desire to serve God soon became filled with deception and distance. It is important to notice, however, that God remained faithful to his promises to Isaac and Rebekah despite their failures.

Isaac and Rebekah's story is told in Genesis 24-28. Both are mentioned in Romans 9:10. Isaac is also referred to in Romans 9:7-8; Hebrews 11:17-20; and James 2:21-24.

STRENGTHS AND ACCOMPLISHMENTS:
- They had a caring and loving marriage—at least until their sons were born.
- They were the recipients of God's promises to Abraham.

WEAKNESSES AND MISTAKES:
- Isaac and Rebekah often allowed the end to justify the means.
- In facing difficult situations, Isaac and Rebekah often lied to avoid the problems they faced.
- Both of them alienated each other by playing favorites with their sons.

LESSONS FROM THEIR LIVES:
- God keeps his promises and remains faithful even when we are faithless.
- God's promises and plans are bigger than we are.
- Playing favorites is harmful in a family.
- Deception is destructive in marriage and other significant relationships.

KEY VERSE:
"And Isaac brought Rebekah into his mother's tent, and she became his wife. He loved her very much, and she was a special comfort to him after the loss of his mother" (Genesis 24:67).

---

²³"Whose daughter are you, miss?" he asked. "Would your father have any room to put us up for the night?"

²⁴"My father is Bethuel," she replied. "My grandparents are Milcah and Nahor. ²⁵Yes, we have plenty of straw and food for the camels, and a guest room."

²⁶The man stood there a moment with head bowed, worshiping Jehovah. ²⁷"Thank you, Lord God of my master Abraham," he prayed; "thank you for being so kind and true to him, and for leading me straight to the family of my master's relatives."

²⁸The girl ran home to tell her folks, ²⁹,³⁰and when her brother Laban saw the ring, and the bracelets on his sister's wrists, and heard her story, he rushed out to the spring where the man was still standing beside his camels, and said to him, ³¹"Come and stay with us, friend; why stand here outside the city when we have a room all ready for you, and a place prepared for the camels!"

³²So the man went home with Laban, and Laban gave him straw to bed down the camels, and feed for them, and water for the camel drivers to wash their feet. ³³Then supper was served. But the old man said, "I don't want to eat until I have told you why I am here."

"All right," Laban said, "tell us your errand."

³⁴"I am Abraham's servant," he explained. ³⁵"And Jehovah has overwhelmed my master with blessings so that he is a great man among the people of his land. God has given him flocks of sheep and herds of cattle, and a fortune in silver and gold, and many slaves and camels and donkeys.

³⁶"Now when Sarah, my master's wife, was very old, she gave birth to my master's son, and my master has given him everything he owns. ³⁷And my master made me promise not to let

Isaac marry one of the local girls, ³⁸but to come to his relatives here in this far-off land, to his brother's family, and to bring back a girl from here to marry his son. ³⁹'But suppose I can't find a girl who will come?' I asked him. ⁴⁰'She will,' he told me—'for my Lord, in whose presence I have walked, will send his angel with you and make your mission successful. Yes, find a girl from among my relatives, from my brother's family. ⁴¹You are under oath to go and ask. If they won't send anyone, then you are freed from your promise.'

⁴²"Well, this afternoon when I came to the spring I prayed this prayer: 'O Jehovah, the God of my master Abraham, if you are planning to make my mission a success, please guide me in this way: ⁴³Here I am, standing beside this spring. I will say to some girl who comes out to draw water, "Please give me a drink of water!" ⁴⁴And she will reply, "Certainly! And I'll water your camels too!" Let that girl be the one you have selected to be the wife of my master's son.'

⁴⁵"Well, while I was still speaking these words, Rebekah was coming along with her water jug upon her shoulder; and she went down to the spring and drew water and filled the jug. I said to her, 'Please give me a drink.' ⁴⁶She quickly lifted the jug down from her shoulder so that I could drink, and told me, 'Certainly, sir, and I will water your camels too!' So she did! ⁴⁷Then I asked her, 'Whose family are you from?' And she told me, 'Nahor's. My father is Bethuel, the son of Nahor and his wife Milcah.' So I gave her the ring and the bracelets. ⁴⁸Then I bowed my head and worshiped and blessed Jehovah, the God of my master Abraham, because he had led me along just the right path to find a girl from the family of my master's brother. ⁴⁹So tell me, yes or no. Will you or won't you be kind to my master and do what is right? When you tell me, then I'll know what my next step should be, whether to move this way or that."

⁵⁰Then Laban and Bethuel replied, "The Lord has obviously brought you here, so what can we say? ⁵¹Take her and go! Yes, let her be the wife of your master's son, as Jehovah has directed."

⁵²At this reply, Abraham's servant fell to his knees before Jehovah. ⁵³Then he brought out jewels set in solid gold and silver for Rebekah,

and lovely clothing; and he gave many valuable presents to her mother and brother. ⁵⁴Then they had supper, and the servant and the men with him stayed there overnight. But early the next morning he said, "Send me back to my master!"

⁵⁵"But we want Rebekah here at least another ten days or so!" her mother and brother exclaimed. "Then she can go."

⁵⁶But he pleaded, "Don't hinder my return; the Lord has made my mission successful, and I want to report back to my master."

⁵⁷"Well," they said, "we'll call the girl and ask her what she thinks."

⁵⁸So they called Rebekah. "Are you willing to go with this man?" they asked her.

And she replied, "Yes, I will go."

⁵⁹So they told her good-bye, sending along the woman who had been her childhood nurse, ⁶⁰and blessed her with this blessing as they parted:

"Our sister,
May you become
The mother of many millions!
May your descendants
Overcome all your enemies."

⁶¹So Rebekah and her servant girls mounted the camels and went with him.

⁶²Meanwhile, Isaac, whose home was in the Negeb, had returned to Beer-lahai-roi. ⁶³One evening as he was taking a walk out in the fields, meditating, he looked up and saw the camels coming. ⁶⁴Rebekah noticed him and quickly dismounted.

⁶⁵"Who is that man walking through the fields to meet us?" she asked the servant.

And he replied, "It is my master's son!" So she covered her face with her veil. ⁶⁶Then the servant told Isaac the whole story.

⁶⁷And Isaac brought Rebekah into his mother's tent, and she became his wife. He loved her very much, and she was a special comfort to him after the loss of his mother.

CHAPTER 25
Abraham Dies

Now Abraham married again. Keturah was his new wife, and she bore him several children: Zimran, Jokshan, Medan, Midian, Ishbak, Shuah. ³Jokshan's two sons were Sheba and Dedan. Dedan's sons were Asshurim, Letu-

24:67 When we lose someone close to us, it is important that we take some time for rebuilding. It is encouraging to notice that, after losing one major family relationship, Isaac found comfort in a new one. As people are taken away from us, God will provide others to give us the support we need to live a healthy and productive life.

ESAU & JACOB

Sibling rivalry is a natural, though sometimes difficult, aspect of family relationships. Brothers, especially those close in age, often don't get along well as children or young adults. But the twins, Esau and Jacob, took this natural conflict to another level of intensity altogether. Fortunately there was reconciliation later in life, though it required considerable emotional and spiritual growth on the part of both.

Actually, the intense rivalry was predicted by God even before the twins were born. And the situation wasn't helped any by the parents playing favorites with their sons. Isaac clearly preferred Esau, while Rebekah favored Jacob. Relationships in this family went from bad to worse when Esau sold Jacob his birthright for the momentary gratification of his hungry stomach.

One event finally shattered the already fragile relationship between these brothers. Jacob deceived his almost blind father into giving him the final blessing that was intended for the firstborn, Esau. Jacob's elaborate scheme, masterminded by his mother, so enraged Esau that he vowed to kill his brother after his father's death. The victim of his own lack of honesty, Jacob fled for his life. He settled with his uncle Laban and soon married his two daughters, Leah and Rachel.

While living with Laban's family, Jacob became the object of his uncle's own deceitful practices. Through this experience, Jacob learned painful lessons regarding the importance of love and honesty. God had been working in Jacob's life, drawing him progressively closer to himself. So with a sure knowledge of God's presence, Jacob became willing to face his past. He set out on the long journey home and, despite his fears, found forgiveness and reconciliation in the waiting embrace of his brother.

STRENGTHS AND ACCOMPLISHMENTS:
- Both were willing to let go of past failures to find a better future.
- Esau grew to the point of being able to forgive after feeling significant disappointment and anger.
- Jacob matured to the point where he could be honest and humbly seek forgiveness.

WEAKNESSES AND MISTAKES:
- Both were intent on having their own way with little thought of how it might affect others.
- Esau sought instant gratification and suffered great losses as a result.
- Jacob was often dishonest and deceitful in his dealings.

LESSONS FROM THEIR LIVES:
- Parents should never play favorites with their children.
- Forgiveness can take place even when deep hurts have been suffered.
- Even habitually deceitful people can face the past and recover their relationships.

KEY VERSE:
"And then Esau ran to meet him [Jacob] and embraced him affectionately and kissed him; and both of them were in tears!" (Genesis 33:4).

The story of Esau and Jacob is told in Genesis 25–33. Both are also mentioned in Malachi 1:2-3; Acts 3:13; Romans 9:10-13; and Hebrews 11:9, 20-21. Esau is referred to in Hebrews 12:16-17, while Jacob is mentioned in Hosea 12:3-5 and Matthew 1:2; 22:32.

---

shim, and Leummim. [4]Midian's sons were Ephah, Epher, Hanoch, Abida, and Eldaah.

[5]Abraham deeded everything he owned to Isaac; [6]however, he gave gifts to the sons of his concubines and sent them off into the east, away from Isaac.

[7,8]Then Abraham died, at the ripe old age of 175, [9,10]and his sons Isaac and Ishmael buried him in the cave of Mach-pelah near Mamre, in the field Abraham had purchased from Ephron the son of Zohar, the Hethite, where Sarah, Abraham's wife, was buried.

[11]After Abraham's death, God poured out rich blessings upon Isaac. (Isaac had now moved south to Beer-lahai-roi in the Negeb.)

[12-15]Here is a list, in the order of their births, of the descendants of Ishmael, who was the son of Abraham and Hagar the Egyptian, Sarah's slave girl: Nebaioth, Kedar, Abdeel, Mibsam, Mishma, Dumah, Massa, Hadad, Tema, Jetur, Naphish, Kedemah. [16]These twelve sons of his became the founders of twelve tribes that bore their names. [17]Ishmael finally died at the age of 137, and joined his ancestors. [18]These descendants of Ishmael were scattered across the country from Havilah to Shur (which is a little way to the northeast of the Egyptian border in the direction of Assyria). And they were constantly at war with one another.

Jacob and Esau Are Born

[19]This is the story of Isaac's children: [20]Isaac was forty years old when he married Rebekah,

the daughter of Bethuel the Aramean from Paddam-aram. Rebekah was the sister of Laban. ²¹Isaac pleaded with Jehovah to give Rebekah a child, for even after many years of marriage she had no children. Then at last she became pregnant. ²²And it seemed as though children were fighting each other inside her!

"I can't endure this," she exclaimed. So she asked the Lord about it.

²³And he told her, "The sons in your womb shall become two rival nations. One will be stronger than the other; and the older shall be a servant of the younger!"

²⁴And sure enough, she had twins. ²⁵The first was born so covered with reddish hair that one would think he was wearing a fur coat! So they called him "Esau." ²⁶Then the other twin was born with his hand on Esau's heel! So they called him Jacob (meaning "Grabber"). Isaac was sixty years old when the twins were born.

Esau Sells His Birthright

²⁷As the boys grew, Esau became a skillful hunter, while Jacob was a quiet sort who liked to stay at home. ²⁸Isaac's favorite was Esau, because of the venison he brought home, and Rebekah's favorite was Jacob.

²⁹One day Jacob was cooking stew when Esau arrived home exhausted from the hunt.

³⁰*Esau:* "Boy, am I starved! Give me a bite of that red stuff there!" (From this came his nickname "Edom," which means "Red Stuff.")

³¹*Jacob:* "All right, trade me your birthright for it!"

³²*Esau:* "When a man is dying of starvation, what good is his birthright?"

³³*Jacob:* "Well then, vow to God that it is mine!"

And Esau vowed, thereby selling all his eldest-son rights to his younger brother. ³⁴Then Jacob gave Esau bread, peas, and stew; so he ate and drank and went on about his business, indifferent to the loss of the rights he had thrown away.

CHAPTER 26
Isaac Deceives Abimelech

Now a severe famine overshadowed the land, as had happened before, in Abraham's time, and so Isaac moved to the city of Gerar where Abimelech, king of the Philistines, lived.

²Jehovah appeared to him there and told him, "Don't go to Egypt. ³Do as I say and stay here in this land. If you do, I will be with you and bless you, and I will give all this land to you and to your descendants, just as I promised Abraham your father. ⁴And I will cause your descendants to become as numerous as the stars! And I will give them all of these lands; and they shall be a blessing to all the nations of the earth. ⁵I will do this because Abraham obeyed my commandments and laws."

⁶So Isaac stayed in Gerar. ⁷And when the men there asked him about Rebekah, he said, "She is my sister!" For he feared for his life if he told them she was his wife; he was afraid they would kill him to get her, for she was very attractive. ⁸But sometime later, King Abimelech, king of the Philistines, looked out of a window and saw Isaac and Rebekah making love.

⁹Abimelech called for Isaac and exclaimed,

25:23 This prenatal prophecy concerning Jacob and Esau portends conflict between the brothers— and it goes beyond just normal sibling rivalry! Unfortunately, the subsequent family history amply bears this out. Sibling rivalry is often very destructive to family relationships and can easily get out of control. Siblings often separate for life, carrying with them years of hard feelings that taint all their other relationships. Reconciliation with those we have hurt is one of the goals of recovery. Let us take steps toward recovering our important relationships.

25:34 Esau traded his rights as a firstborn son for a bowl of stew to fill his empty stomach. He was indifferent to the things in life that were really important. His primary concern was his physical satisfaction, with no thought at all for his future. He hadn't learned how to delay gratification. The lesson Esau needed to learn is very important for all of us in recovery. We need to see things in the long view. If we can picture the positive results of life in recovery, we will be able to give up the momentary pleasures that keep us from getting there.

26:6-11 Children learn from their parents. Unfortunately, they are not selective about what they learn. They don't learn the good things and ignore the bad. These verses demonstrate what Isaac learned from his father, Abraham. Doubtless, he had heard how Abraham had passed Sarah off as his sister to protect himself (12:10-20; 20:1-18). It is amazing how the sinful patterns of our parents are often repeated in our own life. How often our family dysfunctions repeat themselves generation after generation! Isaac would have been wise to tell the truth and trust God to protect him. Trust in God is one weapon we have to fight against destructive family patterns.

"She is your wife! Why did you say she is your sister?"

"Because I was afraid I would be murdered," Isaac replied. "I thought someone would kill me to get her from me."

¹⁰"How could you treat us this way?" Abimelech exclaimed. "Someone might carelessly have raped her, and we would be doomed." ¹¹Then Abimelech made a public proclamation: "Anyone harming this man or his wife shall die."

Isaac Has a Dispute with Abimelech
¹²That year Isaac's crops were tremendous— 100 times the grain he sowed. For Jehovah blessed him. ¹³He was soon a man of great wealth and became richer and richer. ¹⁴He had large flocks of sheep and goats, great herds of cattle, and many servants. And the Philistines became jealous of him. ¹⁵So they filled up his wells with earth—all those dug by the servants of his father Abraham.

¹⁶And King Abimelech asked Isaac to leave the country. "Go somewhere else," he said, "for you have become too rich and powerful for us."

¹⁷So Isaac moved to Gerar Valley and lived there instead. ¹⁸And Isaac redug the wells of his father Abraham, the ones the Philistines had filled after his father's death, and gave them the same names they had had before, when his father had named them. ¹⁹His shepherds also dug a new well in Gerar Valley, and found a gushing underground spring.

²⁰Then the local shepherds came and claimed it. "This is our land and our well," they said, and argued over it with Isaac's herdsmen. So he named the well, "The Well of Argument!" ²¹Isaac's men then dug another well, but again there was a fight over it. So he called it, "The Well of Anger." ²²Abandoning that one, he dug again, and the local residents finally left him alone. So he called it, "The Well of Room Enough for Us at Last!" "For now at last," he said, "the Lord has made room for us and we shall thrive."

Isaac and Abimelech Are Reconciled
²³When he went to Beer-sheba, ²⁴Jehovah appeared to him on the night of his arrival. "I am the God of Abraham your father," he said. "Fear not, for I am with you and will bless you, and will give you so many descendants that they will become a great nation—because of my promise to Abraham, who obeyed me." ²⁵Then Isaac built an altar and worshiped Jehovah; and he settled there, and his servants dug a well.

²⁶One day Isaac had visitors from Gerar. King Abimelech arrived with his advisor, Ahuzzath, and also Phicol, his army commander.

²⁷"Why have you come?" Isaac asked them. "This is obviously no friendly visit, since you kicked me out in a most uncivil way."

²⁸"Well," they said, "we can plainly see that Jehovah is blessing you. We've decided to ask for a treaty between us. ²⁹Promise that you will not harm us, just as we have not harmed you, and in fact, have done only good to you and have sent you away in peace; we bless you in the name of the Lord."

³⁰So Isaac prepared a great feast for them, and they ate and drank in preparation for the treaty ceremonies. ³¹In the morning, as soon as they were up, they each took solemn oaths to seal a nonaggression pact. Then Isaac sent them happily home again.

³²That very same day Isaac's servants came to tell him, "We have found water"—in the well they had been digging. ³³So he named the well, "The Well of the Oath," and the city that grew up there was named "Oath," and is called that to this day.

³⁴Esau, at the age of forty, married a girl named Judith, daughter of Be-eri the Hethite; and he also married Basemath, daughter of Elon the Hethite. ³⁵But Isaac and Rebekah were bitter about his marrying them.

CHAPTER 27
Jacob Deceives Isaac
One day, in Isaac's old age when he was almost blind, he called for Esau his oldest son.

Isaac: "My son?"
Esau: "Yes, father?"
²⁻⁴*Isaac:* "I am an old man now, and expect every day to be my last. Take your bow and arrows out into the fields and get me some venison, and prepare it just the way

26:23-24 Isaac was afraid, and he had good reason to be. He was surrounded by hostile neighbors who greatly outnumbered his household. He didn't have a place to call his own, except the burial site of his parents. He lived in Gerar "by permission," as it were. At this time, God came to Isaac with this soothing message, "Fear not." We may feel as if we don't belong anywhere. We may have forfeited our place in society. It may seem as though there are enemies all around us. But even when things are at their worst, we need to be aware that God is with us, whispering, "Fear not."

I like it—savory and good—and bring it here for me to eat, and I will give you the blessings that belong to you, my first-born son, before I die."

[5]But Rebekah overheard the conversation. So when Esau left for the field to hunt for the venison, [6,7]she called her son Jacob and told him what his father had said to his brother.

[8-10]*Rebekah:* "Now do exactly as I tell you. Go out to the flocks and bring me two young goats, and I'll prepare your father's favorite dish from them. Then take it to your father, and after he has enjoyed it he will bless *you* before his death, instead of Esau!"

[11,12]*Jacob:* "But mother! He won't be fooled that easily. Think how hairy Esau is, and how smooth my skin is! What if my father feels me? He'll think I'm making a fool of him and curse me instead of bless-ing me!"

[13]*Rebekah:* "Let his curses be on me, dear son. Just do what I tell you. Go out and get the goats."

[14]So Jacob followed his mother's instruc-tions, bringing the dressed kids, which she prepared in his father's favorite way. [15]Then she took Esau's best clothes—they were there in the house—and instructed Jacob to put them on. [16] And she made him a pair of gloves from the hairy skin of the young goats, and fastened a strip of the hide around his neck; [17]then she gave him the meat, with its rich aroma, and some fresh-baked bread.

[18]Jacob carried the platter of food into the room where his father was lying.

Jacob: "Father?"
Isaac: "Yes? Who is it, my son—Esau or Jacob?"
[19]*Jacob:* "It's Esau, your oldest son. I've done as you told me to. Here is the delicious venison you wanted. Sit up and eat it, so that you will bless me with all your heart!"

[20]*Isaac:* "How were you able to find it so quickly, my son?"
Jacob: "Because Jehovah your God put it in my path!"
[21]*Isaac:* "Come over here. I want to feel you and be sure it really is Esau!"

[22](Jacob goes over to his father. He feels him!)

Isaac: (to himself) "The voice is Jacob's, but the hands are Esau's!"

[23](The ruse convinces Isaac and he gives Jacob his blessings):

[24]*Isaac:* "Are you really Esau?"
Jacob: "Yes, of course."
[25]*Isaac:* "Then bring me the venison, and I will eat it and bless you with all my heart."

(Jacob takes it over to him and Isaac eats; he also drinks the wine Jacob brings him.)

[26]*Isaac:* "Come here and kiss me, my son!"

(Jacob goes over and kisses him on the cheek. Isaac sniffs his clothes, and finally seems convinced.)

[27-29]*Isaac:* "The smell of my son is the good smell of the earth and fields that Jehovah has blessed. May God always give you plenty of rain for your crops, and good harvests and grapes. May many nations be your slaves. Be the master of your brothers. May all your relatives bow low before you. Cursed are all who curse you, and blessed are all who bless you."

[30](As soon as Isaac has blessed Jacob, and almost before Jacob leaves the room, Esau arrives, coming in from his hunting. [31]He also has prepared his father's favorite dish and brings it to him.)

Esau: "Here I am, father, with the venison. Sit up and eat it so that you can give me your finest blessings!"

27:1-29 It is heartbreaking to watch Rebekah and Jacob conspire to deceive Isaac. Notice the great lengths to which they go to fool the old man. They knew that Jacob was the heir to God's promises through Abraham (see 25:23, 29-33), but through their deceit they were trying to make God's program happen. That never works without causing pain or added trouble somewhere else. God is in charge of the timetable of our recovery program. We need to stick with the truth and move at his pace.

27:33 At this point Isaac realized he had blessed Jacob instead of Esau, but he could not take his blessing back. Jacob would receive the inheritance and blessing of the firstborn son. It became clear that it was God's plan that Jacob should be the recipient of God's promises to Abraham, so Isaac acquiesced to God's will. There are often times when God, through circumstances, will veto our plans. Through grace, he often delivers us from making bad choices and protects us from the terri-ble consequences. As the third step reminds us, we must surrender our will to God if we are to progress in recovery.

[32]*Isaac:* "Who is it?"

Esau: "Why, it's me, of course! Esau, your oldest son!"

[33](Isaac begins to tremble noticeably.)

Isaac: "Then who is it who was just here with venison, and I have already eaten it and blessed him with irrevocable blessing?"

[34](Esau begins to sob with deep and bitter sobs.)

Esau: "O my father, bless me, bless me too!"

[35]*Isaac:* "Your brother was here and tricked me and has carried away your blessing."

[36]*Esau:* (bitterly) "No wonder they call him 'The Cheater.' For he took my birthright, and now he has stolen my blessing. Oh, haven't you saved even one blessing for me?"

[37]*Isaac:* "I have made him your master, and have given him yourself and all of his relatives as his servants. I have guaranteed him abundance of grain and wine—what is there left to give?"

[38]*Esau:* "Not one blessing left for me? O my father, bless me too."

(Isaac says nothing as Esau weeps.)

[39,40]*Isaac:* "Yours will be no life of ease and luxury, but you shall hew your way with your sword. For a time you will serve your brother, but you will finally shake loose from him and be free."

[41]So Esau hated Jacob because of what he had done to him. He said to himself, "My father will soon be gone, and then I will kill Jacob." [42]But someone got wind of what he was planning and reported it to Rebekah. She sent for Jacob and told him that his life was being threatened by Esau.

[43]"This is what to do," she said. "Flee to your Uncle Laban in Haran. [44]Stay there with him awhile until your brother's fury is spent, [45]and he forgets what you have done. Then I will send for you. For why should I be bereaved of both of you in one day?"

[46]Then Rebekah said to Isaac, "I'm sick and tired of these local girls. I'd rather die than see Jacob marry one of them."

CHAPTER 28
Jacob Is Sent to Find a Wife

So Isaac called for Jacob and blessed him and said to him, "Don't marry one of these Canaanite girls. [2]Instead, go at once to Paddan-aram, to the house of your grandfather Bethuel, and marry one of your cousins—your Uncle Laban's daughters. [3]God Almighty bless you and give you many children; may you become a great nation of many tribes! [4]May God pass on to you and to your descendants the mighty blessings promised to Abraham. May you own this land where we now are foreigners, for God has given it to Abraham."

[5]So Isaac sent Jacob away, and he went to Paddan-aram to visit his Uncle Laban, his mother's brother—the son of Bethuel the Aramean.

[6-8]Esau realized that his father despised the local girls, and that his father and mother had sent Jacob to Paddan-aram, with his father's blessing, to get a wife from there, and that they had strictly warned him against marrying a Canaanite girl, and that Jacob had agreed and had left for Paddan-aram. [9]So Esau went to his Uncle Ishmael's family and married another wife from there, besides the wives he already had. Her name was Mahalath, the sister of Nebaioth, and daughter of Ishmael, Abraham's son.

Jacob's Dream and God's Promise

[10]So Jacob left Beer-sheba and journeyed toward Haran. [11]That night, when he stopped to camp at sundown, he found a rock for a headrest and lay down to sleep, [12]and dreamed that a staircase reached from earth to heaven, and he saw the angels of God going up and down upon it.

[13]At the top of the stairs stood the Lord. "I am Jehovah," he said, "the God of Abraham, and of your father, Isaac. The ground you are lying on is yours! I will give it to you and to your descendants. [14]For you will have descendants as many as dust! They will cover the land from east to west and from north to south; and all the nations of the earth will be blessed through you and your descendants. [15]What's more, I am with you, and will protect

---

27:34-40 Here, Esau demonstrates tearful remorse, but according to Hebrews 12:16-17, it was too late. As a young man he had sold his future for instant gratification. Now he had to suffer the consequences for not waiting to fill his hungry stomach. Those of us in recovery know what this is like. Time and again we have chosen to sell our future for immediate satisfaction or for something that will dull the pain we are hiding inside. But even though time has been lost, there is hope for those who are willing to take steps toward recovery.

you wherever you go, and will bring you back safely to this land; I will be with you constantly until I have finished giving you all I am promising."

16,17Then Jacob woke up. "God lives here!" he exclaimed in terror. "I've stumbled into his home! This is the awesome entrance to heaven!" 18The next morning he got up very early and set his stone headrest upright as a memorial pillar, and poured olive oil over it. 19He named the place Bethel ("House of God"), though the previous name of the nearest village was Luz.

20And Jacob vowed this vow to God: "If God will help and protect me on this journey and give me food and clothes, 21and will bring me back safely to my father, then I will choose Jehovah as my God! 22And this memorial pillar shall become a place for worship; and I will give you back a tenth of everything you give me!"

CHAPTER 29
Jacob Meets Rachel
Jacob traveled on, finally arriving in the land of the East. 2He saw in the distance three flocks of sheep lying beside a well in an open field, waiting to be watered. But a heavy stone covered the mouth of the well. 3(The custom was that the stone was not removed until all the flocks were there. After watering them, the stone was rolled back over the mouth of the well again.) 4Jacob went over to the shepherds and asked them where they lived.

"At Haran," they said.

5"Do you know a fellow there named Laban, the son of Nahor?"

"We sure do."

6"How is he?"

"He's well and prosperous. Look, there comes his daughter Rachel with the sheep."

7"Why don't you water the flocks so they can get back to grazing?" Jacob asked. "They'll be hungry if you stop so early in the day!"

8"We don't roll away the stone and begin the watering until all the flocks and shepherds are here," they replied.

9As this conversation was going on, Rachel arrived with her father's sheep, for she was a shepherdess. 10And because she was his cousin—the daughter of his mother's brother—and because the sheep were his uncle's, Jacob went over to the well and rolled away the stone and watered his uncle's flock. 11Then Jacob kissed Rachel and started crying! 12,13He explained about being her cousin on her father's side, and that he was her Aunt Rebekah's son. She quickly ran and told her father, Laban, and as soon as he heard of Jacob's arrival, he rushed out to meet him and greeted him warmly and brought him home. Then Jacob told him his story.

14"Just think, my very own flesh and blood," Laban exclaimed.

Jacob Marries Rachel and Leah
After Jacob had been there about a month, 15Laban said to him one day, "Just because we are relatives is no reason for you to work for me without pay. How much do you want?" 16Now Laban had two daughters, Leah, the older, and her younger sister, Rachel. 17Leah had lovely eyes, but Rachel was shapely, and in every way a beauty. 18Well, Jacob was in love with Rachel. So he told her father, "I'll work for you seven years if you'll give me Rachel as my wife."

19"Agreed!" Laban replied. "I'd rather give her to you than to someone outside the family."

20So Jacob spent the next seven years working to pay for Rachel. But they seemed to him but a few days, he was so much in love. 21Finally the time came for him to marry her.

"I have fulfilled my contract," Jacob said to Laban. "Now give me my wife, so that I can sleep with her."

22So Laban invited all the men of the settlement to celebrate with Jacob at a big party. 23Afterwards, that night, when it was dark, Laban took Leah to Jacob, and he slept with her. 24(And Laban gave to Leah a servant girl, Zilpah, to be her maid.) 25But in the morning—it was Leah!

"What sort of trick is this?" Jacob raged at

28:20-22 Jacob's vow to God here is possibly just another of his schemes—something like a "foxhole" prayer. But even though Jacob was probably trying to "con" God—give him "an offer he couldn't refuse"—God honored and blessed Jacob. God's dealings with Jacob should give us some idea of how gracious he really is. Jacob wasn't exemplary or wise; he didn't know the God of his fathers as he should have. Yet God still was willing to work with him and bless him.
29:25 Jacob's response to Laban's trickery reveals an interesting principle. Nobody resents being cheated more than a cheater. If there is a characteristic in others that we find particularly annoying, we would be wise to examine ourselves. It is probably one of our own.

Laban. "I worked for seven years for Rachel. What do you mean by this trickery?"

²⁶"It's not our custom to marry off a younger daughter ahead of her sister," Laban replied smoothly. ²⁷"Wait until the bridal week is over and you can have Rachel too—if you promise to work for me another seven years!"

²⁸So Jacob agreed to work seven more years. Then Laban gave him Rachel, too. ²⁹And Laban gave to Rachel a servant girl, Bilhah, to be her maid. ³⁰So Jacob slept with Rachel, too, and he loved her more than Leah, and stayed and worked the additional seven years.

Jacob Has Many Children

³¹But because Jacob was slighting Leah, Jehovah let her have a child, while Rachel was barren. ³²So Leah became pregnant and had a son, Reuben (meaning "God has noticed my trouble"), for she said, "Jehovah has noticed my trouble—now my husband will love me." ³³She soon became pregnant again and had another son and named him Simeon (meaning "Jehovah heard"), for she said, "Jehovah heard that I was unloved, and so he has given me another son." ³⁴Again she became pregnant and had a son, and named him Levi (meaning "Attachment") for she said, "Surely now my husband will feel affection for me, since I have given him three sons!" ³⁵Once again she was pregnant and had a son and named him Judah (meaning "Praise"), for she said, "Now I will praise Jehovah!" And then she stopped having children.

CHAPTER 30

Rachel, realizing she was barren, became envious of her sister. "Give me children or I'll die," she exclaimed to Jacob.

²Jacob flew into a rage. "Am I God?" he flared. "He is the one who is responsible for your barrenness."

³Then Rachel told him, "Sleep with my servant-girl Bilhah, and her children will be mine." ⁴So she gave him Bilhah to be his wife, and he slept with her, ⁵and she became pregnant and presented him with a son. ⁶Rachel named him Dan (meaning "Justice"), for she said, "God has given me justice, and heard my plea and given me a son." ⁷Then Bilhah, Rachel's servant-girl, became pregnant again and gave Jacob a second son. ⁸Rachel named

him Naphtali (meaning "Wrestling"), for she said, "I am in a fierce contest with my sister and I am winning!"

⁹Meanwhile, when Leah realized that she wasn't getting pregnant anymore, she gave her servant-girl Zilpah to Jacob, to be his wife, ¹⁰and soon Zilpah presented him with a son. ¹¹Leah named him Gad (meaning "My luck has turned!").

¹²Then Zilpah produced a second son, ¹³and Leah named him Asher (meaning "Happy"), for she said, "What joy is mine! The other women will think me blessed indeed!"

¹⁴One day during the wheat harvest, Reuben found some mandrakes growing in a field and brought them to his mother Leah. Rachel begged Leah to give some of them to her.

¹⁵But Leah angrily replied, "Wasn't it enough to steal my husband? And now will you steal my son's mandrakes too?"

Rachel said sadly, "He will sleep with you tonight because of the mandrakes."

¹⁶That evening as Jacob was coming home from the fields, Leah went out to meet him. "You must sleep with me tonight!" she said; "for I am hiring you with some mandrakes my son has found!" So he did. ¹⁷And God answered her prayers and she became pregnant again, and gave birth to her fifth son. ¹⁸She named him Issachar (meaning "Wages"), for she said, "God has repaid me for giving my slave-girl to my husband." ¹⁹Then once again she became pregnant, with a sixth son. ²⁰She named him Zebulun (meaning "Gifts"), for she said, "God has given me good gifts for my husband. Now he will honor me, for I have given him six sons." ²¹Afterwards she gave birth to a daughter and named her Dinah.

²²Then God remembered about Rachel's plight, and answered her prayers by giving her a child. ²³,²⁴For she became pregnant and gave birth to a son. "God has removed the dark slur against my name," she said. And she named him Joseph (meaning "May I also have another!"), for she said, "May Jehovah give me another son."

Jacob Becomes Wealthy

²⁵Soon after the birth of Joseph to Rachel, Jacob said to Laban, "I want to go back home. ²⁶Let me take my wives and children—for I earned them from you—and be gone, for you

---

30:25-43 God always treated Jacob in ways far better than he deserved. God blessed him in spite of his trickery and deceit. God works that way with us, too. He is willing to bless us with healing even when we don't really deserve it. None of us really deserves God's love; all of us have failed in many ways. But God still reaches out to help us when we look to him in faith.

know how fully I have paid for them with my service to you."

²⁷"Please don't leave me," Laban replied, "for a fortune-teller that I consulted told me that the many blessings I've been enjoying are all because of your being here. ²⁸How much of a raise do you need to get you to stay? Whatever it is, I'll pay it."

²⁹Jacob replied, "You know how faithfully I've served you through these many years, and how your flocks and herds have grown. ³⁰For it was little indeed you had before I came, and your wealth has increased enormously; Jehovah has blessed you from everything I do! But now, what about me? When should I provide for my own family?"

³¹,³²"What wages do you want?" Laban asked again.

Jacob replied, "If you will do one thing, I'll go back to work for you. Let me go out among your flocks today and remove all the goats that are speckled or spotted, and all the black sheep. Give them to me as my wages. ³³Then if you ever find any white goats or sheep in my flock, you will know that I have stolen them from you!"

³⁴"All right!" Laban replied. "It shall be as you have said!"

³⁵,³⁶So that very day Laban went out and formed a flock for Jacob of all the male goats that were ringed and spotted, and the females that were speckled and spotted with any white patches, and all of the black sheep. He gave them to Jacob's sons to take them three days' distance, and Jacob stayed and cared for Laban's flock. ³⁷Then Jacob took fresh shoots from poplar, almond, and sycamore trees, and peeled white streaks in them, ³⁸and placed these rods beside the watering troughs so that Laban's flocks would see them when they came to drink; for that is when they mated. ³⁹,⁴⁰So the flocks mated before the white-streaked rods, and their offspring were streaked and spotted, and Jacob added them to his flock. Then he divided out the ewes from Laban's flock and segregated them from the rams, and let them mate only with Jacob's black rams. Thus he built his flocks from Laban's. ⁴¹Moreover, he watched for the stronger animals to mate, and placed the peeled branches before them, ⁴²but didn't with the feebler ones. So the less healthy lambs were Laban's and the stronger ones were Jacob's! ⁴³As a result, Jacob's flocks increased rapidly and he became very wealthy, with many servants, camels, and donkeys.

CHAPTER 31
Jacob Leaves Laban

But Jacob learned that Laban's sons were grumbling, "He owes everything he owns to our father. All his wealth is at our father's expense." ²Soon Jacob noticed a considerable cooling in Laban's attitude toward him.

³Jehovah now spoke to Jacob and told him, "Return to the land of your fathers, and to your relatives there; and I will be with you."

⁴So one day Jacob sent for Rachel and Leah to come out to the field where he was with the flocks, ⁵to talk things over with them.

"Your father has turned against me," he told them, "and now the God of my fathers has come and spoken to me. ⁶You know how hard I've worked for your father, ⁷but he has been completely unscrupulous and has broken his wage contract with me again and again and again. But God has not permitted him to do me any harm! ⁸For if he said the speckled animals would be mine, then all the flock produced speckled; and when he changed and said I could have the streaked ones, then all the lambs were streaked! ⁹In this way God has made me wealthy at your father's expense.

¹⁰"And at the mating season, I had a dream,

31:3 Moving can be a time of major crisis. It is interesting to note that during all the major change points of Jacob's life, God always reestablished contact with him. Here, as Jacob faced a crisis with Laban's family, God gave Jacob instructions concerning his next move. God revealed to Jacob the next step in his divine program as it was needed. God is always there to help us during our crisis moments. During these times we need to learn to stop and listen to what he has to say.

31:14-15 Leah and Rachel left their father's home willingly. This is not surprising. We have enough evidence to know that Laban's family was highly dysfunctional. At this point, Jacob's family needed to move on if they were to become the family God intended them to be. Sometimes our home of origin is a source of much pain and confusion. In such cases, it is important for us to leave that dysfunctional context in order to build a new life in a more healthy atmosphere.

31:17-20 Even though God was very active in Jacob's life, the old patterns still persisted. Jacob's recovery from his deceitful youth was an ongoing process. This time he deceived Laban. Most of us are in recovery for a lifetime. Jacob's habits and tendencies certainly didn't go away overnight. Neither will ours. We need to be aware of our weaknesses and look to God for his help at each step along the way.

and saw that the he-goats mating with the flock were streaked, speckled, and mottled. [11]Then, in my dream, the Angel of God called to me [12]and told me that I should mate the white female goats with streaked, speckled, and mottled male goats. 'For I have seen all that Laban has done to you,' the Angel said. [13]'I am the God you met at Bethel,' he continued, 'the place where you anointed the pillar and made a vow to serve me. Now leave this country and return to the land of your birth.'"

[14]Rachel and Leah replied, "That's fine with us! There's nothing for us here—none of our father's wealth will come to us anyway! [15]He has reduced our rights to those of foreign women; he sold us, and what he received for us has disappeared. [16]The riches God has given you from our father were legally ours and our children's to begin with! So go ahead and do whatever God has told you to."

Laban Chases after Jacob

[17-20]So one day while Laban was out shearing sheep, Jacob set his wives and sons on camels, and fled without telling Laban his intentions. He drove the flocks before him—Jacob's flocks he had gotten there at Paddan-aram—and took everything he owned and started out to return to his father Isaac in the land of Canaan. [21]So he fled with all of his possessions (and Rachel stole her father's household gods and took them with her) and crossed the Euphrates River and headed for the territory of Gilead.

[22]Laban didn't learn of their flight for three days. [23]Then, taking several men with him, he set out in hot pursuit and caught up with them seven days later, at Mount Gilead. [24]That night God appeared to Laban in a dream.

"Watch out what you say to Jacob," he was told. "Don't give him your blessing and don't curse him." [25]Laban finally caught up with Jacob as he was camped at the top of a ridge; Laban, meanwhile, camped below him in the mountains.

[26]"What do you mean by sneaking off like this?" Laban demanded. "Are my daughters prisoners, captured in a battle, that you have rushed them away like this? [27]Why didn't you give me a chance to have a farewell party, with singing and orchestra and harp? [28]Why didn't you let me kiss my grandchildren and tell them good-bye? This is a strange way to act. [29]I could crush you, but the God of your father appeared to me last night and told me, 'Be careful not to be too hard on Jacob!' [30]But see here—though you feel you must go, and

STEP **10**

Personal Boundaries

BIBLE READING: Genesis 31:45-55

We continued to take personal inventory and when we were wrong promptly admitted it.

We all have particular weaknesses, and it is often helpful to establish personal boundary lines to support these weaker areas. We may need to clearly define our commitments to others; we may need to agree on certain limitations in order to maintain peace. Once the boundaries have been established, honesty is needed to maintain them. An assessment of our honesty in keeping our commitments needs to be part of our regular inventory.

Jacob and his father-in-law, Laban, had some conflicts. As they were working them out, they entered into an agreement by drawing a clearly defined boundary line and setting up a monument to remind them of that commitment. "'May the Lord see to it that we keep this bargain when we are out of each other's sight. . . . This heap [of stones],' Laban continued, 'stands between us as a witness of our vows. . . .' So Jacob took oath before the mighty God of his father, Isaac, to respect the boundary line" (Genesis 31:49, 51-53).

Restoring trust in our relationships is part of recovery. To do this we should define our expectations and cautiously enter into commitments. We are not merely responsible for what the other person knows about. We are personally responsible for our own honesty before the watchful eyes of God. These relational commitments are not to be entered into lightly. But when we make them, they must be vigilantly maintained. *Turn to page 1239, Romans 5.*

long so intensely for your childhood home—why have you stolen my idols?"

³¹"I sneaked away because I was afraid," Jacob answered. "I said to myself, 'He'll take his daughters from me by force.' ³²But as for your household idols, a curse upon anyone who took them. Let him die! If you find a single thing we've stolen from you, I swear before all these men, I'll give it back without question." For Jacob didn't know that Rachel had taken them.

³³Laban went first into Jacob's tent to search there, then into Leah's, and then searched the two tents of the concubines, but didn't find them. Finally he went into Rachel's tent. ³⁴Rachel, remember, was the one who had stolen the idols; she had stuffed them into her camel saddle and now was sitting on them! So although Laban searched the tents thoroughly, he didn't find them.

³⁵"Forgive my not getting up, father," Rachel explained, "but I'm having my monthly period." So Laban didn't find them.

³⁶,³⁷Now Jacob got mad. "What did you find?" he demanded of Laban. "What is my crime? You have come rushing after me as though you were chasing a criminal and have searched through everything. Now put everything I stole out here in front of us, before your men and mine, for all to see and to decide whose it is! ³⁸Twenty years I've been with you, and all that time I cared for your ewes and goats so that they produced healthy offspring, and I never touched one ram of yours for food. ³⁹If any were attacked and killed by wild animals, did I show them to you and ask you to reduce the count of your flock? No, I took the loss. You made me pay for every animal stolen from the flocks, whether I could help it or not. ⁴⁰I worked for you through the scorching heat of the day, and through the cold and sleepless nights. ⁴¹Yes, twenty years—fourteen of them earning your two daughters, and six years to get the flock! And you have reduced my wages ten times! ⁴²In fact, except for the grace of God—the God of my grandfather Abraham, even the glorious God of Isaac, my father—you would have sent me off without a penny

to my name. But God has seen your cruelty and my hard work, and that is why he appeared to you last night."

⁴³Laban replied, "These women are my daughters, and these children are mine, and these flocks and all that you have—all are mine. So how could I harm my own daughters and grandchildren? ⁴⁴Come now and we will sign a peace pact, you and I, and will live by its terms."

⁴⁵So Jacob took a stone and set it up as a monument, ⁴⁶and told his men to gather stones and make a heap, and Jacob and Laban ate together beside the pile of rocks. ⁴⁷,⁴⁸They named it "The Witness Pile"—"Jegar-sahadutha," in Laban's language, and "Galeed" in Jacob's.

"This pile of stones will stand as a witness against us [if either of us trespasses across this line]," Laban said. ⁴⁹So it was also called "The Watchtower" (Mizpah). For Laban said, "May the Lord see to it that we keep this bargain when we are out of each other's sight. ⁵⁰And if you are harsh to my daughters, or take other wives, I won't know, but God will see it. ⁵¹,⁵²This heap," Laban continued, "stands between us as a witness of our vows that I will not cross this line to attack you and you will not cross it to attack me. ⁵³I call upon the God of Abraham and Nahor, and of their father, to destroy either one of us who does."

So Jacob took oath before the mighty God of his father, Isaac, to respect the boundary line. ⁵⁴Then Jacob presented a sacrifice to God there at the top of the mountain, and invited his companions to a feast, and afterwards spent the night with them on the mountain. ⁵⁵Laban was up early the next morning and kissed his daughters and grandchildren, and blessed them, and returned home.

CHAPTER 32
Jacob Reconciles with Esau

So Jacob and his household started on again. And the angels of God came to meet him. When he saw them he exclaimed, "God lives here!" So he named the place "God's territory!"

31:49 This verse is often quoted as a sweet benediction, but, in actuality, it is a very negative wish that becomes almost a threat. It's as if Laban were saying, "I can't watch you anymore, so when you're out of my sight, I pray that God will keep his eye on you, you rascal!"

32:3 Twenty years prior to these events Jacob had run away from Esau afraid for his life. Jacob had no way of knowing whether his brother, Esau, had experienced healing from the old wounds and resentments. Since he did not know, he had to make elaborate preparations for reestablishing contact. Jacob's example in this chapter gives many helpful hints to those of us seeking reconciliation with people we have hurt in the past.

³Jacob now sent messengers to his brother, Esau, in Edom, in the land of Seir, ⁴with this message: "Hello from Jacob! I have been living with Uncle Laban until recently, ⁵and now I own oxen, donkeys, sheep, goats, and many servants, both men and women. I have sent these messengers to inform you of my coming, hoping that you will be friendly to us."

⁶The messengers returned with the news that Esau was on the way to meet Jacob—with an army of 400 men! ⁷Jacob was frantic with fear. He divided his household, along with the flocks and herds and camels, into two groups; ⁸for he said, "If Esau attacks one group, perhaps the other can escape."

⁹Then Jacob prayed, "O God of Abraham my grandfather, and of my father Isaac—O Jehovah who told me to return to the land of my relatives, and said that you would do me good— ¹⁰I am not worthy of the least of all your loving-kindnesses shown me again and again just as you promised me. For when I left home I owned nothing except a walking stick! And now I am two armies! ¹¹O Lord, please deliver me from destruction at the hand of my brother Esau, for I am frightened—terribly afraid that he is coming to kill me and these mothers and my children. ¹²But you promised to do me good, and to multiply my descendants until they become as the sands along the shores—too many to count."

¹³⁻¹⁵Jacob stayed where he was for the night, and prepared a present for his brother Esau: 200 female goats, 20 male goats, 200 ewes, 20 rams, 30 milk camels, with their colts, 40 cows, 10 bulls, 20 female donkeys, 10 male donkeys.

¹⁶He instructed his servants to drive them on ahead, each group of animals by itself, separated by a distance between. ¹⁷He told the men driving the first group that when they met Esau and he asked, "Where are you going? Whose servants are you? Whose animals are these?"— ¹⁸they should reply: "These belong to your servant Jacob. They are a present for his master Esau! He is coming right behind us!"

¹⁹Jacob gave the same instructions to each driver, with the same message. ²⁰Jacob's strategy was to appease Esau with the presents before meeting him face to face! "Perhaps," Jacob hoped, "he will be friendly to us." ²¹So the presents were sent on ahead, and Jacob spent that night in the camp.

²²⁻²⁴But during the night he got up and wakened his two wives and his two concubines and eleven sons, and sent them across the Jordan River at the Jabbok ford with all his

S T E P

9

Long-Awaited Healing

BIBLE READING: Genesis 33:1-11

We made direct amends to such people wherever possible, except when to do so would injure them or others.

Returning to someone we have hurt is a scary thing. The passing years, lack of communication, and memories of anger and hateful emotional exchanges can all create tremendous anxiety. Even though we may make some contact through a third party, there will still be tension until we see that person face to face.

This was the case for Jacob upon returning to see Esau. "Then, far in the distance, Jacob saw Esau coming with his 400 men. . . . Then Jacob went on ahead. . . . And then Esau ran to meet him and embraced him affectionately and kissed him; and both of them were in tears!" After being introduced to Jacob's family, Esau asked, "'And what were all the flocks and herds I met as I came?' . . . Jacob replied, 'They are my gifts, to curry your favor!' 'Brother, I have plenty,' Esau laughed. 'Keep what you have.' 'No, but please accept them,' Jacob said, 'for what a relief it is to see your friendly smile! I was as frightened of you as though approaching God! Please take my gifts. For God has been very generous to me and I have enough.' So Jacob insisted, and finally Esau accepted them" (Genesis 33:1, 3-4, 8-11).

Jacob's tremendous fear gave way to relief. The last time Jacob had seen Esau, Jacob was in fear for his life. With the passing of time, both of them had changed. When Jacob faced his brother, he found that there was still affection, even though they both remembered the pain. *Turn to page 353, 2 Samuel 9.*

possessions, then returned again to the camp and was there alone; and a Man wrestled with him until dawn. ²⁵And when the Man saw that he couldn't win the match, he struck Jacob's hip and knocked it out of joint at the socket.

²⁶Then the Man said, "Let me go, for it is dawn."

But Jacob panted, "I will not let you go until you bless me."

²⁷"What is your name?" the Man asked.

"Jacob," was the reply.

²⁸"It isn't anymore!" the Man told him. "It is Israel—one who has power with God. Because you have been strong with God, you shall prevail with men."

²⁹"What is *your* name?" Jacob asked him.

"No, you mustn't ask," the Man told him. And he blessed him there.

³⁰Jacob named the place "Peniel" ("The Face of God"), for he said, "I have seen God face to face, and yet my life is spared." ³¹The sun rose as he started on, and he was limping because of his hip. ³²(That is why even today the people of Israel don't eat meat from near the hip, in memory of what happened that night.)

CHAPTER 33

Then, far in the distance, Jacob saw Esau coming with his 400 men. ²Jacob now arranged his family into a column, with his two concubines and their children at the head, Leah and her children next, and Rachel and Joseph last. ³Then Jacob went on ahead. As he approached his brother he bowed low seven times before him. ⁴And then Esau ran to meet him and embraced him affectionately and kissed him; and both of them were in tears!

⁵Then Esau looked at the women and children and asked, "Who are these people with you?"

"My children," Jacob replied. ⁶Then the concubines came forward with their children, and bowed low before him. ⁷Next came Leah with her children, and bowed, and finally Rachel and Joseph came and made their bows.

⁸"And what were all the flocks and herds I met as I came?" Esau asked.

And Jacob replied, "They are my gifts, to curry your favor!"

⁹"Brother, I have plenty," Esau laughed. "Keep what you have."

¹⁰"No, but please accept them," Jacob said, "for what a relief it is to see your friendly smile! I was as frightened of you as though approaching God! ¹¹Please take my gifts. For God has been very generous to me and I have enough." So Jacob insisted, and finally Esau accepted them.

¹²"Well, let's be going," Esau said. "My men and I will stay with you and lead the way."

¹³But Jacob replied, "As you can see, some of the children are small, and the flocks and herds have their young, and if they are driven too hard, they will die. ¹⁴So you go on ahead of us and we'll follow at our own pace and meet you at Seir."

¹⁵"Well," Esau said, "at least let me leave you some of my men to assist you and be your guides."

"No," Jacob insisted, "we'll get along just fine. Please do as I suggest."

¹⁶So Esau started back to Seir that same day. ¹⁷Meanwhile Jacob and his household went as far as Succoth. There he built himself a camp, with pens for his flocks and herds. (That is why the place is called Succoth, meaning "huts.") ¹⁸Then they arrived safely at Shechem, in Canaan, and camped outside the city. ¹⁹(He bought the land he camped on from the family of Hamor, Shechem's father, for 100 pieces of silver. ²⁰And there he erected an altar and called it "El-Elohe-Israel," "The Altar to the God of Israel.")

CHAPTER 34

Jacob's Sons Take Revenge

One day Dinah, Leah's daughter, went out to visit some of the neighborhood girls, ²but when Shechem, son of King Hamor the Hivite, saw her, he took her and raped her. ³He fell

---

33:4 Although Esau does seem genuinely delighted to see his long-lost brother, we can only speculate about his true feelings. This happy reunion certainly didn't signal the end of the brothers' feud. Conflict between their families continued throughout Old Testament times. The book of Obadiah records the joy that Esau's descendants, the Edomites, expressed over the Israelites' defeat. Obadiah, an Israelite, also joyfully announced the doom of Edom. Even in the New Testament, the hated family of Herod traced its lineage back to Esau. Some conflicts are not easily resolved but if they are left unresolved, they can become a burden to generations far into the future.

34:2 The act of rape is always hideous in itself, but the consequences are usually just as heartbreaking. In this occurrence, rape led to deception and ultimately to murder. Dysfunctional patterns, and the acts that follow out of them, feed cycles of deepening destruction and hurt. Someone has to choose to break the cycle and begin the process of recovery and healing.

JACOB & SONS

While not the first dysfunctional family in the Bible, Jacob's brood was certainly among the most controversial. Like father, like son, the saying goes. Jacob's own lack of discretion, honesty, patience, and unconditional love negatively impacted his clan.

Jacob had never been his father's favorite, and he tragically played favorites with his own sons. Joseph was obviously preferred; Benjamin ran a close second. The rest were far back in the pack and understandably jealous.

The deceptions that Jacob had put over on his father and brother many years earlier were mirrored in the lies of his sons about the fate of Joseph. As the brutal massacre of Shechem brutally illustrated, openness and honesty didn't characterize the sons' relationships with outsiders either. Jacob's silence at Dinah's rape perhaps spurred Simeon and Levi to seek vengeance on their own. Certainly their father set no clear boundaries on their behavior until it was much too late.

Jacob's polygamy influenced his sons also. Reuben even slept with his father's concubine Bilhah. Why not? He had grown up watching a marital triangle expand to include two servant concubines. He had even been a party to his mother's and Rachel's rivalry for Jacob's favors. He was not the only one to sin sexually. Judah, too, succumbed to temptation with his disguised daughter-in-law, Tamar.

Jacob and his sons did mature significantly over the years. When famine forced them to visit Egypt, they were no longer the selfish, jealous, deceitful band of earlier years. Instead, they were genuinely concerned for their aging father, protective of young Benjamin, and remorseful when confronted with the truth of what they had done to Joseph. The past reconciled, they could begin an exciting new life in Egypt with the brother they had abandoned. They were, to a great extent, worthy to become the forefathers of Israel's twelve tribes. Judah would even head the royal line, with its most famous descendant the King of kings, Jesus Christ.

STRENGTHS AND ACCOMPLISHMENTS:
- In later years the brothers honestly cared about their father.
- They were the forefathers of the twelve tribes of Israel.
- They eventually learned the value of loyalty and honesty.

WEAKNESSES AND MISTAKES:
- Jacob modeled favoritism, impatience, and sexual indiscretion for his sons.
- Unbridled passion and intense jealousy motivated the boys, who found it difficult to establish boundaries for their behavior.
- Honesty was a learned response, acquired rather late in life for Jacob and several of his sons.

LESSONS FROM THEIR LIVES:
- The sins of the parents are often reflected in their children.
- Parental favoritism has devastating consequences.
- God can take the evil in our life and use it to accomplish great good.

KEY VERSE:
"Hurry, return to my father and tell him, 'Your son Joseph says, "God has made me chief of all the land of Egypt. Come down to me right away!"'" (Genesis 45:9).

The story of Jacob and his sons is found in Genesis 34–50. Jacob is also mentioned in Hosea 12:3-5; Matthew 1:2; 22:32; Acts 3:13; 7:46; Romans 9:11-13; and Hebrews 11:9, 20-21.

---

deeply in love with her, and tried to win her affection.

[4]Then he spoke to his father about it. "Get this girl for me," he demanded. "I want to marry her."

[5]Word soon reached Jacob of what had happened, but his sons were out in the fields herding cattle, so he did nothing until their return. [6,7]Meanwhile King Hamor, Shechem's father, went to talk with Jacob, arriving just as Jacob's sons came in from the fields, too shocked and angry to overlook the insult, for it was an outrage against all of them.

[8]Hamor told Jacob, "My son Shechem is truly in love with your daughter, and longs for her to be his wife. Please let him marry her. [9,10]Moreover, we invite you folks to live here among us and to let your daughters marry our sons, and we will give our daughters as wives for your young men. And you shall live among us wherever you wish and carry on your business among us and become rich!"

[11]Then Shechem addressed Dinah's father and brothers. "Please be kind to me and let me have her as my wife," he begged. "I will give whatever you require. [12]No matter what

dowry or gift you demand, I will pay it—only give me the girl as my wife."

[13]Her brothers then lied to Shechem and Hamor, acting dishonorably because of what Shechem had done to their sister. [14]They said, "We couldn't possibly. For you are not circumcised. It would be a disgrace for her to marry such a man. [15]I'll tell you what we'll do—if every man of you will be circumcised, [16]then we will intermarry with you and live here and unite with you to become one people. [17]Otherwise we will take her and be on our way."

[18,19]Hamor and Shechem gladly agreed, and lost no time in acting upon this request, for Shechem was very much in love with Dinah, and could, he felt sure, sell the idea to the other men of the city—for he was highly respected and very popular. [20]So Hamor and Shechem appeared before the city council and presented their request.

[21]"Those men are our friends," they said. "Let's invite them to live here among us and ply their trade. For the land is large enough to hold them, and we can intermarry with them. [22]But they will only consider staying here on one condition—that every one of us men be circumcised, the same as they are. [23]But if we do this, then all they have will become ours and the land will be enriched. Come on, let's agree to this so that they will settle here among us."

[24]So all the men agreed, and all were circumcised. [25]But three days later, when their wounds were sore and sensitive to every move they made, two of Dinah's brothers, Simeon and Levi, took their swords, entered the city without opposition, and slaughtered every man there, [26]including Hamor and Shechem. They rescued Dinah from Shechem's house and returned to their camp again. [27]Then all of Jacob's sons went over and plundered the city because their sister had been dishonored there. [28]They confiscated all the flocks and herds and donkeys—everything they could lay their hands on, both inside the city and outside in the fields, [29]and took all the women and children, and wealth of every kind.

[30]Then Jacob said to Levi and Simeon, "You have made me stink among all the people of this land—all the Canaanites and Perizzites.

We are so few that they will come and crush us, and we will all be killed."

[31]"Should he treat our sister like a prostitute?" they retorted.

CHAPTER 35
Rachel and Isaac Die

"Move on to Bethel now, and settle there," God said to Jacob, "and build an altar to worship me—the God who appeared to you when you fled from your brother Esau."

[2]So Jacob instructed all those in his household to destroy the idols they had brought with them, and to wash themselves and to put on fresh clothing. [3]"For we are going to Bethel," he told them, "and I will build an altar there to the God who answered my prayers in the day of my distress, and was with me on my journey."

[4]So they gave Jacob all their idols and their earrings, and he buried them beneath the oak tree near Shechem. [5]Then they started on again. And the terror of God was upon all the cities they journeyed through, so that they were not attacked. [6]Finally they arrived at Luz (also called Bethel), in Canaan. [7]And Jacob erected an altar there and named it "The altar to the God who met me here at Bethel" because it was there at Bethel that God appeared to him when he was fleeing from Esau.

[8]Soon after this Rebekah's old nurse, Deborah, died and was buried beneath the oak tree in the valley below Bethel. And ever after it was called "The Oak of Weeping."

[9]Upon Jacob's arrival at Bethel, en route from Paddan-aram, God appeared to him once again and blessed him. [10]And God said to him, "You shall no longer be called Jacob ('Grabber'), but Israel ('One who prevails with God'). [11]I am God Almighty," the Lord said to him, "and I will cause you to be fertile and to multiply and to become a great nation, yes, many nations; many kings shall be among your descendants. [12]And I will pass on to you the land I gave to Abraham and Isaac. Yes, I will give it to you and to your descendants."

[13,14]Afterwards Jacob built a stone pillar at the place where God had appeared to him; and he poured wine over it as an offering to God and then anointed the pillar with olive

---

34:20-31 Vengeance belongs to God and when an individual takes revenge—no matter how just the cause may be—there usually are serious consequences. Because of their deception and slaughter of the Hivites, Jacob and his family became extremely unpopular with their neighbors. Because they were a small clan at this point, such a situation presented them with grave danger. In recovery, revenge is extremely counterproductive. It only breaks down the reconciliation process that is necessary for personal growth and healthy relationships.

oil. [15]Jacob named the spot Bethel ("House of God"), because God had spoken to him there.

[16]Leaving Bethel, he and his household traveled on toward Ephrath (Bethlehem). But Rachel's pains of childbirth began while they were still a long way away. [17]After a very hard delivery, the midwife finally exclaimed, "Wonderful—another boy!" [18]And with Rachel's last breath (for she died) she named him "Ben-oni" ("Son of my sorrow"); but his father called him "Benjamin" ("Son of my right hand").

[19]So Rachel died, and was buried near the road to Ephrath (also called Bethlehem). [20]And Jacob set up a monument of stones upon her grave, and it is there to this day.

[21]Then Israel journeyed on and camped beyond the Tower of Eder. [22]It was while he was there that Reuben slept with Bilhah, his father's concubine, and someone told Israel about it.

Here are the names of the twelve sons of Jacob:

[23]The sons of Leah: Reuben, Jacob's oldest child, Simeon, Levi, Judah, Issachar, Zebulun.

[24]The sons of Rachel: Joseph, Benjamin.

[25]The sons of Bilhah, Rachel's servant-girl: Dan, Naphtali.

[26]The sons of Zilpah, Leah's servant-girl: Gad, Asher.

All these were born to him at Paddan-aram.

[27]So Jacob came at last to Isaac his father at Mamre in Kiriath-arba (now called Hebron), where Abraham too had lived. [28,29]Isaac died soon afterwards, at the ripe old age of 180. And his sons Esau and Jacob buried him.

CHAPTER 36
Esau's Family
Here is a list of the descendants of Esau (also called Edom): [2,3]Esau married three local girls from Canaan: Adah (daughter of Elon the Hethite), Oholibamah (daughter of Anah and granddaughter of Zibeon the Hivite), Basemath (his cousin—she was a daughter of Ishmael—the sister of Nebaioth).

[4]Esau and Adah had a son named Eliphaz. Esau and Basemath had a son named Reuel.

[5]Esau and Oholibamah had sons named Jeush, Jalam, and Korah. All these sons were born to Esau in the land of Canaan.

[6-8]Then Esau took his wives, children, household servants, cattle and flocks—all the wealth he had gained in the land of Canaan—and moved away from his brother Jacob to Mount Seir. (For there was not land enough to support them both because of all their cattle.)

[9]Here are the names of Esau's descendants, the Edomites, born to him in Mount Seir:

[10-12]Descended from his wife Adah, born to her son Eliphaz were: Teman, Omar, Zepho, Gatam, Kenaz, Amalek (born to Timna, Eliphaz' concubine).

[13,14]Esau also had grandchildren from his wife Basemath. Born to her son Reuel were: Nahath, Zerah, Shammah, Mizzah.

[15,16]Esau's grandchildren became the heads of clans, as listed here: the clan of Teman, the clan of Omar, the clan of Zepho, the clan of Kenaz, the clan of Korah, the clan of Gatam, the clan of Amalek.

The above clans were the descendants of Eliphaz, the oldest son of Esau and Adah.

[17]The following clans were the descendants of Reuel, born to Esau and his wife Basemath while they lived in Canaan: the clan of Nahath, the clan of Zerah, the clan of Shammah, the clan of Mizzah.

[18,19]And these are the clans named after the sons of Esau and his wife Oholibamah (daughter of Anah): the clan of Jeush, the clan of Jalam, the clan of Korah.

[20,21]These are the names of the tribes that descended from Seir, the Horite—one of the native families of the land of Seir: the tribe of Lotan, the tribe of Shobal, the tribe of Zibeon, the tribe of Anah, the tribe of Dishon, the tribe of Ezer, the tribe of Dishan.

[22]The children of Lotan (the son of Seir) were Hori and Heman. (Lotan had a sister, Timna.)

35:22 The families in the book of Genesis seem to be inordinately dysfunctional. Deceit and lies are often used for the sake of convenience. Communication between family members is poor. The incidence of incest is high. Here we see that Reuben slept with one of his father's wives. This kind of sexual sin reaps a bitter harvest. Reuben's blessing and inheritance as the firstborn son was forfeited because of this single act of sexual gratification (49:4). Reuben needed to keep the long view in focus. If he had thought about what he might lose, he might have withstood the temptation.

36:6-8 Esau and his family could not live in the same area as Jacob and his family. The excuse they gave for moving was the lack of land available. For some families, no amount of room is enough for them to live together. The reconciliation of these brothers was started, but it seems never to have been completed. We need to expect reconciliation to take time. It doesn't happen with one happy reunion. It needs to be worked out over a period of time, in the everyday situations of life.

²³The children of Shobal: Alvan, Manahath, Ebal, Shepho, Onam.

²⁴The children of Zibeon: Aiah, Anah. (This is the boy who discovered a hot springs in the wasteland while he was grazing his father's donkeys.)

²⁵The children of Anah: Dishon, Oholibamah.

²⁶The children of Dishon: Hemdan, Eshban, Ithran, Cheran.

²⁷The children of Ezer: Bilhan, Zaavan, Akan.

²⁸⁻³⁰ The children of Dishan: Uz, Aran.

³¹⁻³⁹These are the names of the kings of Edom (before Israel had her first king):

King Bela (son of Beor), from Dinhabah in Edom.
Succeeded by: King Jobab (son of BoZerah), from the city of Bozrah.
Succeeded by: King Husham, from the land of the Temanites.
Succeeded by: King Hadad (son of Bedad), the leader of the forces that defeated the army of Midian when it invaded Moab. His city was Avith.
Succeeded by: King Samlah, from Masrekah.
Succeeded by: King Shaul, from Rehoboth-by-the-River.
Succeeded by: King Baal-hanan (son of Achbor).
Succeeded by: King Hadad, from the city of Pau.

King Hadad's wife was Mehetabel, daughter of Matred and granddaughter of Mezahab.

⁴⁰⁻⁴³Here are the names of the sub-tribes of Esau, living in the localities named after themselves: the clan of Timna, the clan of Alvah, the clan of Jetheth, the clan of Oholibamah, the clan of Elah, the clan of Pinon, the clan of Kenaz, the clan of Teman, the clan of Mibzar, the clan of Magdiel, the clan of Iram.

These, then, are the names of the subtribes of Edom, each giving its name to the area it occupied. (All were Edomites, descendants of Esau.)

CHAPTER 37
Joseph's Dreams

So Jacob settled again in the land of Canaan, where his father had lived.

²Jacob's son Joseph was now seventeen years old. His job, along with his half brothers, the sons of his father's wives Bilhah and Zilpah, was to shepherd his father's flocks. But Joseph reported to his father some of the bad things they were doing. ³Now as it happened, Israel loved Joseph more than any of his other children, because Joseph was born to him in his old age. So one day Jacob gave him a special gift—a brightly colored coat. ⁴His brothers of course noticed their father's partiality, and consequently hated Joseph; they couldn't say a kind word to him. ⁵One night Joseph had a dream and promptly reported the details to his brothers, causing even deeper hatred.

⁶"Listen to this," he proudly announced. ⁷"We were out in the field binding sheaves, and my sheaf stood up, and your sheaves all gathered around it and bowed low before it!"

⁸"So you want to be our king, do you?" his brothers derided. And they hated him both for the dream and for his cocky attitude.

⁹Then he had another dream and told it to his brothers. "Listen to my latest dream," he boasted. "The sun, moon, and eleven stars bowed low before me!" ¹⁰This time he told his father as well as his brothers; but his father rebuked him. "What is this?" he asked. "Shall I indeed, and your mother and brothers come and bow before you?" ¹¹His brothers were fit to be tied concerning this affair, but his father gave it quite a bit of thought and wondered what it all meant.

Joseph Is Sold into Egypt

¹²One day Joseph's brothers took their father's flocks to Shechem to graze them there. ¹³,¹⁴A few days later Israel called for Joseph, and told

---

37:3 The biblical account does not hide the fact that Joseph was Jacob's favorite son. Joseph had no choice but to accept the blessings of his distinction, along with its accompanying sufferings. It is interesting to note that the pattern of parental favoritism did not start with the life Joseph. It had been played out in the lives of his father Jacob and his grandfather Isaac as well. It is never healthy for parents to play favorites among their children, but it is a common pattern in dysfunctional families. It is a pattern that causes untold suffering many generations down the road.
37:19-20 The terrible impact of jealousy is portrayed in this passage. The brothers are now at the point of planning Joseph's murder. They almost followed through on their plan, but cooler heads prevailed. They ended up selling Joseph into slavery and then lying to their father, Jacob. Here we see the tragic, cumulative effects of the dysfunctional patterns of deceit and favoritism in the family context.

GOD grant me the serenity
to accept the things I cannot change
the courage to change the things I can
and the wisdom to know the difference AMEN

There are times when life just treats us unfairly. We may protest the injustices, fall victim to self-pity, give in to a "poor me" kind of attitude, or sink into depression. During these times when life is unfair, we really need serenity.

If anyone in history could claim to have been treated unfairly, it was Joseph. He was one of twelve brothers, the favorite of his father. In their jealousy, the ten older brothers staged his death to fool their father and sold Joseph into slavery in Egypt. Once a slave, Joseph devoted himself to serving his master well and was quickly promoted. He was then propositioned by his master's wife, and when Joseph refused her, he was falsely accused of rape. Thrown into prison, and with no hope of release, he again did his best to serve. He was soon running the administration of the prison. In the end, after many long years, Joseph was freed. He was promoted to the position of prime minister of Egypt. From this position Joseph was able to confront and forgive his brothers who had sold him into slavery many years before (Genesis 37–45).

It takes serenity, courage, and wisdom to maintain a healthy attitude when life isn't fair. We can't change the fact that our world is imperfect and things are far from the way they should be, but we can choose the attitude we will take. We need serenity from God to help us change our response to the injustices of life. We need courage to face with optimism the days when we are treated unfairly. We need wisdom to know whether to fight injustice or to make the best of a bad situation. *Turn to page 231, Joshua 1.*

him, "Your brothers are over in Shechem grazing the flocks. Go and see how they are getting along, and how it is with the flocks, and bring me word."

"Very good," Joseph replied. So he traveled to Shechem from his home at Hebron Valley. [15]A man noticed him wandering in the fields.

"Who are you looking for?" he asked.

[16]"For my brothers and their flocks," Joseph replied. "Have you seen them?"

[17]"Yes," the man told him, "they are no longer here. I heard your brothers say they were going to Dothan." So Joseph followed them to Dothan and found them there. [18]But when they saw him coming, recognizing him in the distance, they decided to kill him!

[19,20]"Here comes that master dreamer," they exclaimed. "Come on, let's kill him and toss him into a well and tell Father that a wild animal has eaten him. Then we'll see what will become of all his dreams!"

[21,22]But Reuben hoped to spare Joseph's life. "Let's not kill him," he said; "we'll shed no blood—let's throw him alive into this well here; that way he'll die without our touching him!" (Reuben was planning to get him out later and return him to his father.) [23]So when Joseph got there, they pulled off his brightly colored robe, [24]and threw him into an empty well—there was no water in it. [25]Then they sat down for supper. Suddenly they noticed a string of camels coming towards them in the distance, probably Ishmaelite traders who were taking gum, spices, and herbs from Gilead to Egypt.

[26,27]"Look there," Judah said to the others. "Here come some Ishmaelites. Let's sell Joseph to them! Why kill him and have a guilty conscience? Let's not be responsible for his death, for, after all, he is our brother!" And his brothers agreed. [28]So when the traders came by, his brothers pulled Joseph out of the well and sold

him to them for twenty pieces of silver, and they took him along to Egypt. ²⁹Some time later, Reuben (who was away when the traders came by) returned to get Joseph out of the well. When Joseph wasn't there, he ripped at his clothes in anguish and frustration.

³⁰"The child is gone; and I, where shall I go now?" he wept to his brothers. ³¹Then the brothers killed a goat and spattered its blood on Joseph's coat, ³²and took the coat to their father and asked him to identify it.

"We found this in the field," they told him. "Is it Joseph's coat or not?" ³³Their father recognized it at once.

"Yes," he sobbed, "it is my son's coat. A wild animal has eaten him. Joseph is without doubt torn in pieces."

³⁴Then Israel tore his garments and put on sackcloth and mourned for his son in deepest mourning for many weeks. ³⁵His family all tried to comfort him, but it was no use.

"I will die in mourning for my son," he would say, and then break down and cry.

³⁶Meanwhile, in Egypt, the traders sold Joseph to Potiphar, an officer of the Pharaoh—the king of Egypt. Potiphar was captain of the palace guard, the chief executioner.

CHAPTER 38
Judah and Tamar

About this time, Judah left home and moved to Adullam and lived there with a man named Hirah. ²There he met and married a Canaanite girl—the daughter of Shua. ³⁻⁵They lived at Chezib and had three sons, Er, Onan, and Shelah. These names were given to them by their mother, except for Er, who was named by his father.

⁶When his oldest son, Er, grew up, Judah arranged for him to marry a girl named Tamar. ⁷But Er was a wicked man, and so the Lord killed him.

⁸Then Judah said to Er's brother, Onan, "You must marry Tamar, as our law requires of a dead man's brother; so that her sons from you will be your brother's heirs."

⁹But Onan was not willing to have a child who would not be counted as his own, and so, although he married her, whenever he went in to sleep with her, he spilled the sperm on the bed to prevent her from having a baby which would be his brother's. ¹⁰So far as the Lord was concerned, it was very wrong of him [to deny a child to his deceased brother], so he killed him, too. ¹¹Then Judah told Tamar, his daughter-in-law, not to marry again at that time, but to return to her childhood home and to her parents, and to remain a widow there until his youngest son, Shelah, was old enough to marry her. (But he didn't really intend for Shelah to do this, for fear God would kill him, too, just as he had his two brothers.) So Tamar went home to her parents.

¹²In the process of time Judah's wife died. After the time of mourning was over, Judah

---

37:31-35 All Jacob's life he had manipulated people and circumstances to serve his own purposes. He was a schemer and a trickster. Here we see the trickster being tricked once again—by his sons. Again we see a destructive family pattern being passed on to the next generation.

38:1-5 We are told that Judah moved from his family home, married a Canaanite girl, and settled down among them. Some of Judah's unsavory activities in this chapter seem out of sync with what we might expect of one of Israel's patriarchs. We cannot help but wonder whether some of his behavior was not influenced by the people he was living with. The Canaanites were known for their immoral life-style. For us to progress in recovery we need to spend time with people who will encourage us to develop a wholesome life-style. We may also need to give up the relationships that lead us into destructive activities.

38:1-30 Judah's more sensational sin of propositioning a prostitute often blinds readers to his primary failure. According to the laws practiced at the time, if a husband died before fathering a son, his family was responsible for providing his widow with a husband. This was Judah's responsibility, but when his second son died soon after marrying Tamar, Judah was understandably shaken and delayed giving her his third son. It seems that Judah was hoping he would never be called upon to carry out his duty. His attitude didn't solve the problem, but only led to the sordid events that followed. It is easy for us to act like Judah, ignoring our problems or blaming them on our environment or other people. But the first step in solving any problem is admitting we have it. Then we can take responsible steps to solve it.

38:12-26 When Judah failed to deal with Tamar in a responsible way, Tamar decided to take action. And though not everything she did was exemplary, she wisely confronted Judah in a way that caught his attention without alienating him. Very often direct confrontation with people who have wronged us will only deepen the conflict. In such cases, a less direct means of communication may prove helpful.

JUDAH & TAMAR

Judah was the fourth and last son of Leah, Jacob's first wife. Among the patriarch's twelve sons, Judah evidently occupied a position of prominence. Early on in the biblical story, he persuaded his brothers not to kill Joseph. And when they went to Egypt for food, Judah spoke and acted on his brothers' behalf. Later the royal line would come through the descendants of Judah. Tamar was a girl of Canaanite descent, chosen by Judah to be the wife of Er, his oldest son.

As the story of Judah begins, we are told he left his childhood home and moved some distance away from his brothers. He settled in a Canaanite community and married a Canaanite girl. Judah's wife gave birth to three sons: Er, Onan, and Shelah. Er was said to be evil in God's sight and after marrying Tamar, God punished him with death. Onan, as Tamar's brother-in-law, was expected to give her a son who could carry on Er's name and receive his inheritance. But Onan refused to fulfill his responsibility and suffered the same fate as his older brother.

Now it was left to young Shelah to raise up offspring for Er and Onan. But Judah was afraid that his last son would also die. So he told Tamar to return to her father's house until Shelah was older. Judah's intent seemed clear: Shelah would eventually fulfill his duty as a brother-in-law and have a son with Tamar. Time passed and Tamar's expectations were not fulfilled. So she took matters into her own hands, assumed the guise of a prostitute, and tricked Judah into getting her pregnant.

When Judah heard Tamar was pregnant, he demanded her punishment as any self-respecting father-in-law would do. But she showed Judah the items he had given as a pledge, proving that he was the father of the child. So Judah acknowledged that he was in the wrong. Tamar later gave birth to two sons, one of whom is named in the kingly lineage of David, and of Jesus the Messiah.

STRENGTHS AND ACCOMPLISHMENTS:
- After being confronted, Judah admitted his failures and took responsibility for them.

WEAKNESSES AND MISTAKES:
- Judah lost close contact with the patriarchal family, perhaps weakening his resolve to do right.
- Judah failed to fulfill his paternal responsibilities toward Tamar.
- Judah let fear dictate his actions, perhaps indicating his lack of faith.
- Tamar failed to confront Judah directly, resorting to indirect manipulation.

LESSONS FROM THEIR LIVES:
- A shallow walk with God can lead to trouble in family relationships.
- Commitments made to others, whether stated or implied, must be kept.
- God's grace can bring future blessings out of our biggest mistakes.
- Tactful confrontation is needed when legitimate expectations have not been fulfilled.

KEY VERSE:
"Judah . . . said, 'She [Tamar] is more in the right than I am, because I refused to keep my promise to give her to my son Shelah.' But he did not marry her" (Genesis 38:26).

The story of Judah and Tamar is told in Genesis 38. Judah is mentioned in Genesis 29–50 and throughout the Old Testament as one of the fathers of the twelve tribes. Judah and Tamar are both mentioned in Jesus' family tree in Matthew 1.

---

and his friend Hirah, the Adullamite, went to Timnah to supervise the shearing of his sheep. ¹³When someone told Tamar that her father-in-law had left for the sheep shearing at Timnah, ¹⁴and realizing by now that she was not going to be permitted to marry Shelah, though he was fully grown, she laid aside her widow's clothing and covered herself with a veil to disguise herself, and sat beside the road at the entrance to the village of Enaim, which is on the way to Timnah. ¹⁵Judah noticed her as he went by and thought she was a prostitute, since her face was veiled. ¹⁶So he stopped and propositioned her to sleep with him, not realizing of course that she was his own daughter-in-law.

"How much will you pay me?" she asked.

¹⁷"I'll send you a young goat from my flock," he promised.

"What pledge will you give me, so that I can be sure you will send it?" she asked.

¹⁸"Well, what do you want?" he inquired.

"Your identification seal and your walking stick," she replied. So he gave them to her and she let him come and sleep with her; and she became pregnant as a result. ¹⁹Afterwards she resumed wearing her widow's clothing as usual. ²⁰Judah asked his friend Hirah the Adullamite to take the young goat back to her, and to pick up the pledges he had given her, but Hirah couldn't find her!

²¹So he asked around of the men of the city, "Where does the prostitute live who was soliciting out beside the road at the entrance of the village?"

"But we've never had a public prostitute here," they replied. ²²So he returned to Judah and told him he couldn't find her anywhere, and what the men of the place had told him.

²³"Then let her keep them!" Judah exclaimed. "We tried our best. We'd be the laughingstock of the town to go back again."

²⁴About three months later word reached Judah that Tamar, his daughter-in-law, was pregnant, obviously as a result of prostitution.

"Bring her out and burn her," Judah shouted.

²⁵But as they were taking her out to kill her she sent this message to her father-in-law: "The man who owns this identification seal and walking stick is the father of my child. Do you recognize them?"

²⁶Judah admitted that they were his and said, "She is more in the right than I am, because I refused to keep my promise to give her to my son Shelah." But he did not marry her.

²⁷In due season the time of her delivery arrived and she had twin sons. ²⁸As they were being born, the midwife tied a scarlet thread around the wrist of the child who appeared first, ²⁹but he drew back his hand and the other baby was actually the first to be born. "Where did *you* come from!" she exclaimed. And ever after he was called Perez (meaning "Bursting Out"). ³⁰Then, soon afterwards, the baby with the scarlet thread on his wrist was born, and he was named Zerah.

CHAPTER 39
Joseph Serves Potiphar

When Joseph arrived in Egypt as a captive of the Ishmaelite traders, he was purchased from them by Potiphar, a member of the personal staff of Pharaoh, the king of Egypt. Now this man Potiphar was the captain of the king's bodyguard and his chief executioner. ²The Lord greatly blessed Joseph there in the home of his master, so that everything he did succeeded. ³Potiphar noticed this and realized that the Lord was with Joseph in a very special way. ⁴So Joseph naturally became quite a favorite with him. Soon he was put in charge of the administration of Potiphar's household, and all of his business affairs. ⁵At once the Lord began blessing Potiphar for Joseph's sake. All his household affairs began to run smoothly, his crops flourished and his flocks multiplied. ⁶So Potiphar gave Joseph the complete administrative responsibility over everything he owned. He hadn't a worry in the world with Joseph there, except to decide what he wanted to eat! Joseph, by the way, was a very handsome young man.

⁷One day at about this time Potiphar's wife

39:2 God blessed Joseph even in the worst of circumstances. Even as a slave in a strange household and in a foreign land, God made Joseph a success. It should not be inferred that God will also make us successful. Rather, our chief goal should be to follow Joseph's example of being faithful to God's program, no matter what the consequences.

39:7-18 Joseph withstood the temptation of Potiphar's wife even though he was far from home and the temptation continued day after day. This was not a one-time crisis, but a constant, wearing temptation. How did he stand up to it? Two things seem to have helped: Joseph's respect for his master; and even more important, Joseph's respect for God. As we draw closer to God, we will begin to sense his presence in our life. Doing something that runs counter to his program will cause us pain. Walking close to God will provide us with added protection against the temptations we face.

39:19-20 It seems as if the good guys often finish last—the innocent seem to suffer. It looks as though Joseph's faithfulness to God was rewarded with years in prison. This may have discouraged Joseph, but it didn't stop him. Even in prison he continued living according to God's program. In the end, after a number of setbacks, he was rewarded. We may need to look past difficult present circumstances to see that God may have a purpose in our suffering. It may be an important part of our education for future success.

40:1-8 Here we see how Joseph's consistency gained the respect and trust of his jailer and his fellow prisoners. One can imagine that the normal prisoner then, as now, was a pretty sullen character. This makes Joseph's acceptance by them even more significant. His behavior in prison clearly exemplifies the first three steps in recovery. Joseph recognized his powerlessness over the situation he was in and committed his situation to God.

began making eyes at Joseph, and suggested that he come and sleep with her.

⁸Joseph refused. "Look," he told her, "my master trusts me with everything in the entire household; ⁹he himself has no more authority here than I have! He has held back nothing from me except you yourself because you are his wife. How can I do such a wicked thing as this? It would be a great sin against God."

¹⁰But she kept on with her suggestions day after day, even though he refused to listen, and kept out of her way as much as possible. ¹¹Then one day as he was in the house going about his work—as it happened, no one else was around at the time—¹²she came and grabbed him by the sleeve demanding, "Sleep with me." He tore himself away, but as he did, his jacket slipped off and she was left holding it as he fled from the house. ¹³When she saw that she had his jacket, and that he had fled, ¹⁴,¹⁵she began screaming; and when the other men around the place came running in to see what had happened, she was crying hysterically. "My husband had to bring in this Hebrew slave to insult us!" she sobbed. "He tried to rape me, but when I screamed, he ran, and forgot to take his jacket."

¹⁶She kept the jacket, and when her husband came home that night, ¹⁷she told him her story.

"That Hebrew slave you've had around here tried to rape me, ¹⁸and I was only saved by my screams. He fled, leaving his jacket behind!"

¹⁹Well, when her husband heard his wife's story, he was furious. ²⁰He threw Joseph into prison, where the king's prisoners were kept in chains. ²¹But the Lord was with Joseph there, too, and was kind to him by granting him favor with the chief jailer. ²²In fact, the jailer soon handed over the entire prison administration to Joseph, so that all the other prisoners were responsible to him. ²³The chief jailer had no more worries after that, for Joseph took care of everything, and the Lord was with him so that everything ran smoothly and well.

CHAPTER 40
Joseph Interprets Two Dreams
Some time later it so happened that the king of Egypt became angry with both his chief baker and his chief butler, so he jailed them both in the prison where Joseph was, in the castle of Potiphar, the captain of the guard, who was the chief executioner. ⁴They remained under arrest there for quite some

sᵀᴱᴾ 5

Overcoming Denial
BIBLE READING: Genesis 38:1-30
We admitted to God, to ourselves, and to another human being the exact nature of our wrongs.
Admitting our wrongs to ourself can be the most difficult part of Step Five. Denial can be blinding! How can we be expected to admit to ourself those things we are blind to? Here's a clue that can help us. We will often condemn in others the wrongs most deeply hidden within ourself.

According to ancient Jewish law, a widow was entitled to marry the surviving brother of her husband in order to produce children. Tamar had been married successively to two brothers who died without giving her children. Her father-in-law, Judah, promised to give her his youngest son also, but he never did. This left her alone and destitute. In an effort to protect herself, she disguised herself as a prostitute and became pregnant by Judah himself. And she kept his identification seal, which he had given her as a pledge for payment (Genesis 38:1-23).

When Judah heard that Tamar was pregnant and unmarried, he demanded her execution. "But as they were taking her out to kill her she sent this message to her father-in-law: 'The man who owns this identification . . . is the father of my child. Do you recognize them?' Judah admitted that they were his and said, 'She is more in the right than I am'" (Genesis 38:25-26).

It won't be easy to be honest with ourself. "The heart is the most deceitful thing there is, and desperately wicked" (Jeremiah 17:9). However, we can look at those things we condemn in others as a clue to what may be lurking within ourself. *Turn to page 927, Hosea 11.*

time, and Potiphar assigned Joseph to wait on them. ⁵One night each of them had a dream. ⁶The next morning Joseph noticed that they looked dejected and sad.

⁷"What in the world is the matter?" he asked.

⁸And they replied, "We both had dreams last night, but there is no one here to tell us what they mean."

"Interpreting dreams is God's business," Joseph replied. "Tell me what you saw."

⁹,¹⁰The butler told his dream first. "In my dream," he said, "I saw a vine with three branches that began to bud and blossom, and soon there were clusters of ripe grapes. ¹¹I was holding Pharaoh's wine cup in my hand, so I took the grapes and squeezed the juice into it, and gave it to him to drink."

¹²"I know what the dream means," Joseph said. "The three branches mean three days! ¹³Within three days Pharaoh is going to take you out of prison and give you back your job again as his chief butler. ¹⁴And please have some pity on me when you are back in his favor, and mention me to Pharaoh, and ask him to let me out of here. ¹⁵For I was kidnapped from my homeland among the Hebrews, and now this—here I am in jail when I did nothing to deserve it."

¹⁶When the chief baker saw that the first dream had such a good meaning, he told his dream to Joseph, too.

"In my dream," he said, "there were three baskets of pastries on my head. ¹⁷In the top basket were all kinds of bakery goods for Pharaoh, but the birds came and ate them."

¹⁸,¹⁹"The three baskets mean three days," Joseph told him. "Three days from now Pharaoh will take off your head and impale your body on a pole, and the birds will come and pick off your flesh!"

²⁰Pharaoh's birthday came three days later, and he held a party for all of his officials and household staff. He sent for his chief butler and chief baker, and they were brought to him from the prison. ²¹Then he restored the chief butler to his former position; ²²but he sentenced the chief baker to be impaled, just as Joseph had predicted. ²³Pharaoh's wine taster, however, promptly forgot all about Joseph, never giving him a thought.

CHAPTER 41
Joseph Becomes Ruler of Egypt

One night two years later, Pharaoh dreamed that he was standing on the bank of the Nile River, ²when suddenly, seven sleek, fat cows came up out of the river and began grazing in the grass. ³Then seven other cows came up from the river, but they were very skinny and all their ribs stood out. They went over and stood beside the fat cows. ⁴Then the skinny cows ate the fat ones! At which point, Pharaoh woke up!

⁵Soon he fell asleep again and had a second dream. This time he saw seven heads of grain on one stalk, with every kernel well formed and plump. ⁶Then, suddenly, seven more heads appeared on the stalk, but these were shriveled and withered by the east wind. ⁷And these thin heads swallowed up the seven plump, well-formed heads! Then Pharaoh woke up again and realized it was all a dream. ⁸Next morning, as he thought about it, he became very concerned as to what the dreams might mean; he called for all the magicians and sages of Egypt and told them about it, but not one of them could suggest what his dreams meant.⁹Then the king's wine taster spoke up. "Today I remember my sin!" he said. ¹⁰"Some time ago when you were angry with a couple of us and put me and the chief baker in jail in the castle of the captain of the guard, ¹¹the chief baker and I each had a dream one night. ¹²We told the dreams to a young Hebrew fellow there who was a slave of the captain of the guard, and he told us what our dreams meant. ¹³And everything happened just as he said: I was restored to my position of wine taster, and the chief baker was executed, and impaled on a pole."

¹⁴Pharaoh sent at once for Joseph. He was brought hastily from the dungeon, and after

---

40:23 After prophesying the wine taster's release, Joseph must have felt disappointed when he was forgotten. But here again, Joseph refused to play the victim. He didn't poison his life by complaining and assigning blame. He didn't give up and grow bitter. Instead, he continued to live a life that was faithful to God and his plan.

41:14 At last Joseph was given the opportunity for freedom. God's perfect timing had come. We may get discouraged by our slow progress, but we need to faithfully follow God the best we can. Someday we may find we are truly free of the things that bind us. If we experience such deliverance, we can then rejoice. For many of us, however, our dependencies will haunt us throughout this life. If we find ourselves in this situation, we can still rejoice, knowing that through it all we are building a deeper relationship with God.

JOSEPH & BROTHERS

Overconfidence is usually viewed as a negative personality trait. The youthful boasting that Joseph displayed with his brothers was no exception to the rule. His claims that the others would someday bow down to him coupled with his father's favoritism led to jealousy and broken family relationships. In the end, his brothers sold him into slavery, cutting him off from his family altogether.

Through years of difficulties and suffering, Joseph's overconfidence was developed by God into a mature self-assurance. In times of personal struggle, this self-assurance, along with his personal knowledge of God, enabled Joseph to ask, "What shall I do now?" instead of "Why me God?"

Joseph's self-assurance made him capable of tackling and succeeding at jobs that most other people would have run away from. His high personal integrity, refined throughout his life, took him from the bottom of the social ladder to the top. Because of this, Joseph was in a position to save the young nation of Israel during a time of terrible famine.

Overconfidence without God's perspective will invariably lead us down the pathway to many other personal problems and mistakes. On the other hand, self-assurance linked with a strong faith in God will enable us to overcome the many obstacles we face in life.

STRENGTHS AND ACCOMPLISHMENTS:
- Joseph was elevated from slavery to the position of prime minister.
- He had high personal integrity.
- He was a man of great spiritual sensitivity.
- He enabled a nation to prepare for a seven-year famine.

WEAKNESSES AND MISTAKES:
- When he was a young man, his overconfidence severely damaged his family relationships.

LESSONS FROM HIS LIFE:
- Our responses to the circumstances we face are more important than the circumstances themselves.
- God can mold our weaknesses into strengths.
- God can cause situations that others intended for evil to be used for good.

KEY VERSE:
"Turning to Joseph, Pharaoh said to him, 'Since God has revealed the meaning of the dreams to you, you are the wisest man in the country!'" (Genesis 41:39).

Joseph's story is told in Genesis 37–50. Joseph is also mentioned in Acts 7:9-18 and Hebrews 11:22.

---

a quick shave and change of clothes, came in before Pharaoh.

¹⁵"I had a dream last night," Pharaoh told him, "and none of these men can tell me what it means. But I have heard that you can interpret dreams, and that is why I have called for you."

¹⁶"I can't do it by myself," Joseph replied, "but God will tell you what it means!"

¹⁷So Pharaoh told him the dream. "I was standing upon the bank of the Nile River," he said, ¹⁸"when suddenly, seven fat, healthy-looking cows came up out of the river and began grazing along the river bank. ¹⁹But then seven other cows came up from the river, very skinny and bony—in fact, I've never seen such poor-looking specimens in all the land of Egypt. ²⁰And these skinny cattle ate up the seven fat ones that had come out first, ²¹and afterwards they were still as skinny as before! Then I woke up.

²²"A little later I had another dream. This time there were seven heads of grain on one stalk, and all seven heads were plump and full. ²³Then, out of the same stalk, came seven withered, thin heads. ²⁴And the thin heads swallowed up the fat ones! I told all this to my magicians, but not one of them could tell me the meaning."

²⁵"Both dreams mean the same thing," Joseph told Pharaoh. "God was telling you what he is going to do here in the land of Egypt. ²⁶The seven fat cows (and also the seven fat, well-formed heads of grain) mean that there are seven years of prosperity ahead. ²⁷The seven skinny cows (and also the seven thin and withered heads of grain) indicate that there will be seven years of famine following the seven years of prosperity.

²⁸"So God has showed you what he is about to do: ²⁹The next seven years will be a period of great prosperity throughout all the land of Egypt; ³⁰but afterwards there will be seven years of famine so great that all the prosperity will be forgotten and wiped out; famine will consume the land. ³¹The famine will be so terrible that even the memory of the good years will be erased. ³²The double dream gives double impact, showing that what I have told you is certainly going to happen, for God has

decreed it, and it is going to happen soon. ³³My suggestion is that you find the wisest man in Egypt and put him in charge of administering a nationwide farm program. ³⁴,³⁵Let Pharaoh divide Egypt into five administrative districts, and let the officials of these districts gather into the royal storehouses all the excess crops of the next seven years, ³⁶so that there will be enough to eat when the seven years of famine come. Otherwise, disaster will surely strike."

³⁷Joseph's suggestions were well received by Pharaoh and his assistants. ³⁸As they discussed who should be appointed for the job, Pharaoh said, "Who could do it better than Joseph? For he is a man who is obviously filled with the Spirit of God." ³⁹Turning to Joseph, Pharaoh said to him, "Since God has revealed the meaning of the dreams to you, you are the wisest man in the country! ⁴⁰I am hereby appointing you to be in charge of this entire project. What you say goes, throughout all the land of Egypt. I alone will outrank you."

⁴¹,⁴²Then Pharaoh placed his own signet ring on Joseph's finger as a token of his authority, and dressed him in beautiful clothing and placed the royal gold chain about his neck and declared, "See, I have placed you in charge of all the land of Egypt."

⁴³Pharaoh also gave Joseph the chariot of his second-in-command, and wherever he went the shout arose, "Kneel down!" ⁴⁴And Pharaoh declared to Joseph, "I, the king of Egypt, swear that you shall have complete charge over all the land of Egypt."

⁴⁵Pharaoh gave him a name meaning "He has the godlike power of life and death!" And he gave him a wife, a girl named Asenath, daughter of Potiphera, priest of Heliopolis. So Joseph became famous throughout the land of Egypt. ⁴⁶He was thirty years old as he entered the service of the king. Joseph went out from the presence of Pharaoh and began traveling all across the land.

⁴⁷And sure enough, for the next seven years there were bumper crops everywhere. ⁴⁸During those years, Joseph requisitioned for the government a portion of all the crops grown throughout Egypt, storing them in nearby cities. ⁴⁹After seven years of this, the granaries were full to overflowing, and there was so much that no one kept track of the amount.

⁵⁰During this time before the arrival of the first of the famine years, two sons were born to Joseph by Asenath, the daughter of Potiphera, priest of the sun god Re of Heliopolis. ⁵¹Joseph named his oldest son Manasseh (meaning "Made to Forget"—what he meant was that God had made up to him for all the anguish of his youth, and for the loss of his father's home). ⁵²The second boy was named Ephraim (meaning "Fruitful"—"For God has made me fruitful in this land of my slavery," he said).

⁵³So at last the seven years of plenty came to an end. ⁵⁴Then the seven years of famine began, just as Joseph had predicted. There were crop failures in all the surrounding countries, too, but in Egypt there was plenty of grain in the storehouses. ⁵⁵The people began to starve. They pleaded with Pharaoh for food, and he sent them to Joseph. "Do whatever he tells you to," he instructed them.

⁵⁶,⁵⁷So now, with severe famine all over the world, Joseph opened up the storehouses and sold grain to the Egyptians and to those from other lands who came to Egypt to buy grain from Joseph.

CHAPTER 42
Joseph's Brothers Buy Grain

When Jacob heard that there was grain available in Egypt he said to his sons, "Why are you standing around looking at one another? ²I have heard that there is grain available in Egypt. Go down and buy some for us before we all starve to death."

³So Joseph's ten older brothers went down to Egypt to buy grain. ⁴However, Jacob wouldn't let Joseph's younger brother Benjamin go with them, for fear some harm might happen to him [as it had to his brother Joseph]. ⁵So it was that Israel's sons arrived in Egypt along with many others from many lands to buy food, for the famine was as severe in Canaan as it was everywhere else.

⁶Since Joseph was governor of all Egypt, and in charge of the sale of the grain, it was to

---

41:38-40 The primary quality that Pharaoh mentioned about Joseph was his dependence on God. He ignored the fact that Joseph had a questionable past, colored by rumors and a long prison term. Pharaoh could see that God's Spirit was in Joseph, making him a very wise young man. This more than made up for any questions Pharaoh might have had about his past. So Pharaoh promoted Joseph to be the prime minister of Egypt! Some of us may believe that our past has destroyed any hope of a prosperous future. But when we give ourselves to God, asking for his help, no past is too terrible or dark to overcome.

him that his brothers came, and bowed low before him, with their faces to the earth. [7]Joseph recognized them instantly, but pretended he didn't.

"Where are you from?" he demanded roughly.

"From the land of Canaan," they replied. "We have come to buy grain."

[8,9]Then Joseph remembered the dreams of long ago! But he said to them, "You are spies. You have come to see how destitute the famine has made our land."

[10]"No, no," they exclaimed. "We have come to buy food. [11]We are all brothers and honest men, sir! We are not spies!"

[12]"Yes, you are," he insisted. "You have come to see how weak we are."

[13]"Sir," they said, "there are twelve of us brothers, and our father is in the land of Canaan. Our youngest brother is there with our father, and one of our brothers is dead."

[14]"So?" Joseph asked. "What does that prove? You are spies. [15]This is the way I will test your story: I swear by the life of Pharaoh that you are not going to leave Egypt until this youngest brother comes here. [16]One of you go and get your brother! I'll keep the rest of you here, bound in prison. Then we'll find out whether your story is true or not. If it turns out that you don't have a younger brother, then I'll know you are spies."

[17]So he threw them all into jail for three days.

[18]The third day Joseph said to them, "I am a God-fearing man and I'm going to give you an opportunity to prove yourselves. [19]I'm going to take a chance that you are honorable; only one of you shall remain in chains in jail, and the rest of you may go on home with grain for your families; [20]but bring your youngest brother back to me. In this way I will know whether you are telling me the truth; and if you are, I will spare you." To this they agreed.

[21]Speaking among themselves, they said,

"This has all happened because of what we did to Joseph long ago. We saw his terror and anguish and heard his pleadings, but we wouldn't listen."

[22]"Didn't I tell you not to do it?" Reuben asked. "But you wouldn't listen. And now we are going to die because we murdered him."

[23]Of course they didn't know that Joseph understood them as he was standing there, for he had been speaking to them through an interpreter. [24]Now he left the room and found a place where he could weep. Returning, he selected Simeon from among them and had him bound before their eyes. [25]Joseph then ordered his servants to fill the men's sacks with grain, but also gave secret instructions to put each brother's payment at the top of his sack! He also gave them provisions for their journey. [26]So they loaded up their donkeys with the grain and started for home. [27]But when they stopped for the night and one of them opened his sack to get some grain to feed the donkeys, there was his money in the mouth of the sack!

[28]"Look," he exclaimed to his brothers, "my money is here in my sack." They were filled with terror. Trembling, they exclaimed to each other. "What is this that God has done to us?" [29]So they came to their father, Jacob, in the land of Canaan and told him all that had happened.

[30]"The king's chief assistant spoke very roughly to us," they told him, "and took us for spies. [31]'No, no,' we said, 'we are honest men, not spies. [32]We are twelve brothers, sons of one father; one is dead, and the youngest is with our father in the land of Canaan.' [33]Then the man told us, 'This is the way I will find out if you are what you claim to be. Leave one of your brothers here with me and take grain for your families and go on home, [34]but bring your youngest brother back to me. Then I shall know whether you are spies or honest men; if you prove to be what you say, then I

42:7-20 When Joseph recognized his brothers, he took some time to test them. He wanted to discover something of their attitudes before he revealed himself to them. In recovery we are told to work toward reconciliation with the important people in our life. We need wisdom from God to do this in a way that will bring healing to both ourselves and the people close to us. Joseph didn't instantly jump back into a relationship with his brothers. He took the time he needed to do it in a wise way.

42:21-22 After many years Joseph's brothers were still haunted by their guilty conscience. They had sold their brother into Egypt with no plans of ever seeing him again—and no hope of reconciliation or forgiveness. We may wonder how many times during those years Reuben said, "I told you so." It is clear that this period had been one of misery for the brothers. A necessary step in our recovery is seeking reconciliation with others we have wronged. Only then can we experience the healing we need to live a healthy and peaceful life.

will give you back your brother and you can come as often as you like to purchase grain.'"

35As they emptied out the sacks, there at the top of each was the money paid for the grain! Terror gripped them, as it did their father.

36Then Jacob exclaimed, "You have bereaved me of my children—Joseph didn't come back, Simeon is gone, and now you want to take Benjamin too! Everything has been against me."

37Then Reuben said to his father, "Kill my two sons if I don't bring Benjamin back to you. I'll be responsible for him."

38But Jacob replied, "My son shall not go down with you, for his brother Joseph is dead and he alone is left of his mother's children. If anything should happen to him, I would die."

CHAPTER 43
Joseph's Brothers Return to Egypt

But there was no relief from the terrible famine throughout the land. 2When the grain they had brought from Egypt was almost gone, their father said to them, "Go again and buy us a little food."

3-5But Judah told him, "The man wasn't fooling one bit when he said, 'Don't ever come back again unless your brother is with you.' We cannot go unless you let Benjamin go with us."

6"Why did you ever tell him you had another brother?" Israel moaned. "Why did you have to treat me like that?"

7"But the man specifically asked us about our family," they told him. "He wanted to know whether our father was still living and he asked us if we had another brother, so we told him. How could we know that he was going to say, 'Bring me your brother'?"

8Judah said to his father, "Send the lad with me and we will be on our way; otherwise we will all die of starvation—and not only we, but you and all our little ones. 9I guarantee his safety. If I don't bring him back to you, then let me bear the blame forever. 10For we could have gone and returned by this time if you had let him come."

11So their father Israel finally said to them, "If it can't be avoided, then at least do this.

Load your donkeys with the best products of the land. Take them to the man as gifts—balm, honey, spices, myrrh, pistachio nuts, and almonds. 12Take double money so that you can pay back what was in the mouths of your sacks, as it was probably someone's mistake, 13and take your brother and go. 14May God Almighty give you mercy before the man, so that he will release Simeon and return Benjamin. And if I must bear the anguish of their deaths, then so be it."

15So they took the gifts and double money and went to Egypt, and stood before Joseph. 16When Joseph saw that Benjamin was with them, he said to the manager of his household, "These men will eat with me this noon. Take them home and prepare a big feast." 17So the man did as he was told and took them to Joseph's palace. 18They were badly frightened when they saw where they were being taken.

"It's because of the money returned to us in our sacks," they said. "He wants to pretend we stole it and seize us as slaves, with our donkeys."

19As they arrived at the entrance to the palace, they went over to Joseph's household manager, 20and said to him, "O sir, after our first trip to Egypt to buy food, 21as we were returning home, we stopped for the night and opened our sacks, and the money was there that we had paid for the grain. Here it is; we have brought it back again, 22along with additional money to buy more grain. We have no idea how the money got into our sacks."

23"Don't worry about it," the household manager told them; "your God, even the God of your fathers, must have put it there, for we collected your money all right."

Then he released Simeon and brought him out to them. 24They were then conducted into the palace and given water to refresh their feet; and their donkeys were fed. 25Then they got their presents ready for Joseph's arrival at noon, for they were told that they would be eating there. 26When Joseph came home they gave him their presents, bowing low before him.

27He asked how they had been getting along. "And how is your father—the old man you spoke about? Is he still alive?"

42:36 How bitter with grief had Jacob become! He had harbored years of resentment and sadness. His relationship with his sons was built on dishonesty. Walls of lies had been built up—layer upon layer. This separated Jacob from close fellowship with his family. He was all alone in his grief, trapped by the fear that he might lose yet another son. Yet even though Jacob was alone and helpless in his pain, God had a plan for his deliverance. He would soon be set free from many years of bitterness and grief.

28"Yes," they replied. "He is alive and well." Then again they bowed before him.

29Looking at his brother Benjamin, he asked, "Is this your youngest brother, the one you told me about? How are you, my son? God be gracious to you." 30Then Joseph made a hasty exit, for he was overcome with love for his brother and had to go out and cry. Going into his bedroom, he wept there. 31Then he washed his face and came out, keeping himself under control. "Let's eat," he said.

32Joseph ate by himself, his brothers were served at a separate table, and the Egyptians at still another; for Egyptians despise Hebrews and never eat with them. 33He told each of them where to sit, and seated them in the order of their ages, from the oldest to the youngest, much to their amazement! 34Their food was served to them from his own table. He gave the largest serving to Benjamin—five times as much as to any of the others! They had a wonderful time bantering back and forth, and the wine flowed freely!

CHAPTER 44 •
Joseph Tests His Brothers
When his brothers were ready to leave, Joseph ordered his household manager to fill each of their sacks with as much grain as they could carry—and to put into the mouth of each man's sack the money he had paid! 2He was also told to put Joseph's own silver cup at the top of Benjamin's sack, along with the grain money. So the household manager did as he was told. 3The brothers were up at dawn and on their way with their loaded donkeys.

4But when they were barely out of the city, Joseph said to his household manager, "Chase after them and stop them and ask them why they are acting like this when their benefactor has been so kind to them? 5Ask them, 'What do you mean by stealing my lord's personal silver drinking cup, which he uses for fortune telling? What a wicked thing you have done!'" 6So he caught up with them and spoke to them along the lines he had been instructed.

7"What in the world are you talking about?" they demanded. "What kind of people do you think we are, that you accuse us of such a terrible thing as that? 8Didn't we bring back the money we found in the mouth of our sacks? Why would we steal silver or gold from your master's house? 9If you find his cup with any one of us, let that one die. And all the rest of us will be slaves forever to your master."

10"Fair enough," the man replied, "except that only the one who stole it will be a slave, and the rest of you can go free."

11They quickly took down their sacks from the backs of their donkeys and opened them. 12He began searching the oldest brother's sack, going on down the line to the youngest. And the cup was found in Benjamin's! 13They ripped their clothing in despair, loaded the donkeys again, and returned to the city.14Joseph was still home when Judah and his brothers arrived, and they fell to the ground before him.

15"What were you trying to do?" Joseph demanded. "Didn't you know such a man as I would know who stole it?"

16And Judah said, "Oh, what shall we say to my lord? How can we plead? How can we prove our innocence? God is punishing us for our sins. Sir, we have all returned to be your slaves, both we and he in whose sack the cup was found."

17"No," Joseph said. "Only the man who stole the cup, he shall be my slave. The rest of you can go on home to your father."

18Then Judah stepped forward and said, "O sir, let me say just this one word to you. Be patient with me for a moment, for I know you can doom me in an instant, as though you were Pharaoh himself.

19"Sir, you asked us if we had a father or a brother, 20and we said, 'Yes, we have a father, an old man, and a child of his old age, a little one. And his brother is dead, and he alone is left of his mother's children, and his father loves him very much.' 21And you said to us, 'Bring him here so that I can see him.' 22But we said to you, 'Sir, the lad cannot leave his father, for his father would die.' 23But you told us, 'Don't come back here unless your youngest brother is with you.' 24So we returned to our father and told him what you had said. 25And when he said, 'Go back again and buy

---

44:18-34 Judah stepped forward to plead for Benjamin's freedom, fearing what his enslavement would do to Jacob, their father. Many years earlier, the brothers had chosen to sell Joseph into slavery, just for reasons of personal hatred. This had caused their father deep pain. But here, Judah was willing to put himself on the line for his grieving father. Judah and his brothers had grown up a great deal over the years. They had learned from their past mistakes and proved to Joseph that they were ready for reconciliation with their long lost brother.

us a little food,' ²⁶we replied, 'We can't, unless you let our youngest brother go with us. Only then may we come.'

²⁷"Then my father said to us, 'You know that my wife had two sons, ²⁸and that one of them went away and never returned—doubtless torn to pieces by some wild animal; I have never seen him since. ²⁹And if you take away his brother from me also, and any harm befalls him, I shall die with sorrow.' ³⁰And now, sir, if I go back to my father and the lad is not with us—seeing that our father's life is bound up in the lad's life— ³¹when he sees that the boy is not with us, our father will die; and we will be responsible for bringing down his gray hairs with sorrow to the grave. ³²Sir, I pledged my father that I would take care of the lad. I told him, 'If I don't bring him back to you, I shall bear the blame forever.' ³³Please sir, let me stay here as a slave instead of the lad, and let the lad return with his brothers. ³⁴For how shall I return to my father if the lad is not with me? I cannot bear to see what this would do to him."

CHAPTER 45
Joseph Forgives His Brothers
Joseph could stand it no longer.

"Out, all of you," he cried out to his attendants, and he was left alone with his brothers. ²Then he wept aloud. His sobs could be heard throughout the palace, and the news was quickly carried to Pharaoh's palace.

³"I am Joseph!" he said to his brothers. "Is my father still alive?" But his brothers couldn't say a word, they were so stunned with surprise.

⁴"Come over here," he said. So they came closer. And he said again, "I am Joseph, your brother whom you sold into Egypt! ⁵But don't be angry with yourselves that you did this to me, for God did it! He sent me here ahead of you to preserve your lives. ⁶These two years of famine will grow to seven, during which there will be neither plowing nor harvest. ⁷God has sent me here to keep you and your families alive, so that you will become a great nation. ⁸Yes, it was God who sent me here, not you! And he has made me a counselor to Pharaoh, and manager of this entire nation, ruler of all the land of Egypt.

⁹"Hurry, return to my father and tell him, 'Your son Joseph says, "God has made me chief of all the land of Egypt. Come down to me right away! ¹⁰You shall live in the land of Goshen so that you can be near me with all your children, your grandchildren, your flocks and herds, and all that you have. ¹¹,¹²I will take care of you there'" (you men are witnesses of my promise, and my brother Benjamin has heard me say it) "'for there are still five years of famine ahead of us. Otherwise you will come to utter poverty along with all your household.'" ¹³Tell our father about all my power here in Egypt, and how everyone obeys me. And bring him to me quickly."

¹⁴Then, weeping with joy, he embraced Benjamin and Benjamin began weeping too. ¹⁵And he did the same with each of his brothers, who finally found their tongues! ¹⁶The news soon reached Pharaoh—"Joseph's brothers have come"; and Pharaoh was very happy to hear it, as were his officials.

¹⁷Then Pharaoh said to Joseph, "Tell your brothers to load their pack animals and return quickly to their homes in Canaan, ¹⁸and to bring your father and all of your families and come here to Egypt to live. Tell them, 'Pharaoh will assign to you the very best territory in the land of Egypt. You shall live off the fat of the land!' ¹⁹And tell your brothers to take wagons from Egypt to carry their wives and little ones, and to bring your father here. ²⁰Don't worry about your property, for the best of all the land of Egypt is yours."

²¹So Joseph gave them wagons, as Pharaoh had commanded, and provisions for the journey, ²²and he gave each of them new clothes—but to Benjamin he gave five changes of clothes and three hundred pieces of silver! ²³He sent his father ten donkey-loads of the

---

45:1-3 Joseph finally revealed himself to his brothers. For him it was a beautiful reunion, because he had experienced healing by walking with God. But for his brothers, excluding Benjamin, hidden guilt had burdened them for a long time. They were terrified when they recognized Joseph. It is terrifying to open long-hidden guilt to the light, but this is the only road to reconciliation and peace.

45:4-7 Joseph told his brothers not to be angry at themselves for the mistakes they had made in the past. It was now time to rejoice in the present! This was true forgiveness. Joseph was able to see how God had used their mistake to save thousands of lives, including their own. God often turns past disasters into opportunities for great success. When we begin to see that God is working in our life, we will be better able to forgive the people who have wronged us in the past. And if we can see how God has turned around the lives of people we have wronged, we will begin to understand how much God wants our guilt removed and our relationships reconciled.

good things of Egypt, and ten donkeys loaded with grain and all kinds of other food, to eat on his journey. ²⁴So he sent his brothers off.

"Don't quarrel along the way!" was his parting shot! ²⁵And leaving, they returned to the land of Canaan, to Jacob their father.

²⁶"Joseph is alive," they shouted to him. "And he is ruler over all the land of Egypt!" But Jacob's heart was like a stone; he couldn't take it in. ²⁷But when they had given him Joseph's messages, and when he saw the wagons filled with food that Joseph had sent him, his spirit revived.

²⁸And he said, "It must be true! Joseph my son is alive! I will go and see him before I die."

CHAPTER 46
Jacob Moves to Egypt
So Israel set out with all his possessions, and came to Beer-sheba, and offered sacrifices there to the God of his father, Isaac. ²During the night God spoke to him in a vision.

"Jacob! Jacob!" he called.

"Yes?" Jacob answered.

³,⁴"I am God," the voice replied, "the God of your father. Don't be afraid to go down to Egypt, for I will see to it that you become a great nation there. And I will go down with you into Egypt and I will bring your descendants back again; but you shall die in Egypt with Joseph at your side."

⁵So Jacob left Beer-sheba, and his sons brought him to Egypt, along with their little ones and their wives, in the wagons Pharaoh had provided for them. ⁶They brought their livestock, too, and all their belongings accumulated in the land of Canaan, and came to Egypt—Jacob and all his children, ⁷sons and daughters, grandsons and granddaughters— all his loved ones.

⁸⁻¹⁴Here are the names of his sons and grandchildren who went with him into Egypt:

Reuben, his oldest son;
Reuben's sons: Hanoch, Pallu, Hezron, and Carmi.

Simeon and his sons: Jemuel, Jamin, Ohad, Jachin, Zohar, and Shaul (Shaul's mother was a girl from Canaan).
Levi and his sons: Gershon, Kohath, Merari.
Judah and his sons: Er, Onan, Shelah, Perez, Zerah (however, Er and Onan died while still in Canaan, before Israel went to Egypt).
The sons of Perez were Hezron and Hamul.
Issachar and his sons: Tola, Puvah, Iob, Shimron.
Zebulun and his sons: Sered, Elon, Jahleel.

¹⁵So these descendants of Jacob and Leah, not including their daughter Dinah, born to Jacob in Paddan-aram, were thirty-three in all.

¹⁶,¹⁷Also accompanying him were:

Gad and his sons: Ziphion, Haggi, Shuni, Ezbon, Eri, Arodi, and Areli.
Asher and his sons: Imnah, Ishvah, Ishvi, Beriah, and a sister, Serah.
Beriah's sons were Heber and Malchiel.

¹⁸These sixteen persons were the sons of Jacob and Zilpah, the slave-girl given to Leah by her father, Laban.

¹⁹⁻²²Also in the total of Jacob's household were these fourteen sons and descendants of Jacob and Rachel:

Joseph and Benjamin;
Joseph's sons, born in the land of Egypt, were Manasseh and Ephraim (their mother was Asenath, the daughter of Potiphera, priest of Heliopolis);
Benjamin's sons: Bela, Becher, Ashbel, Gera, Naaman, Ehi, Rosh, Muppim, Huppim, and Ard.

²³⁻²⁵Also in the group were these seven sons and descendants of Jacob and Bilhah, the slave-girl given to Rachel by her father, Laban:

Dan and his son: Hushim.
Naphtali and his sons: Jahzeel, Guni, Jezer, and Shillem.

45:24 Joseph knew his brothers so well; he knew they were inclined to argue. Even though Joseph's brothers had matured a great deal since he had last seen them, they still had a long way to go. Deeply ingrained attitudes and habits are hard to get rid of. It all takes time. Joseph's parting shot here shows that he had a sense of humor. But it also reveals that he accepted his brothers as they were, arguments and all.

46:1-4 Some might think it was wrong for the Hebrews to leave the Promised Land, but God's promise to Jacob here shows that God approved of this family reunion in Egypt. When our life is subject to God's authority, where and when we go are up to him. God often uses surprising means to work his will. Notice that God brought Jacob and his family to Egypt for their preservation and growth.

26So the total number of those going to Egypt, of his own descendants, not counting the wives of Jacob's sons, was sixty-six. 27With Joseph and his two sons included, this total of Jacob's household there in Egypt totaled seventy.

28Jacob sent Judah on ahead to tell Joseph that they were on the way, and would soon arrive in Goshen—which they did. 29Joseph jumped into his chariot and journeyed to Goshen to meet his father and they fell into each other's arms and wept a long while.

30Then Israel said to Joseph, "Now let me die, for I have seen you again and know you are alive."

31And Joseph said to his brothers and to all their households, "I'll go and tell Pharaoh that you are here, and that you have come from the land of Canaan to join me. 32And I will tell him, 'These men are shepherds. They have brought with them their flocks and herds and everything they own.' 33So when Pharaoh calls for you and asks you about your occupation, 34tell him, 'We have been shepherds from our youth, as our fathers have been for many generations.' When you tell him this, he will let you live here in the land of Goshen." For shepherds were despised and hated in other parts of Egypt.

CHAPTER 47

Upon their arrival, Joseph went in to see Pharaoh.

"My father and my brothers are here from Canaan," he reported, "with all their flocks and herds and possessions. They wish to settle in the land of Goshen."

2He took five of his brothers with him, and presented them to Pharaoh.

3Pharaoh asked them, "What is your occupation?"

And they replied, "We are shepherds like our ancestors. 4We have come to live here in Egypt, for there is no pasture for our flocks in Canaan—the famine is very bitter there. We request permission to live in the land of Goshen."

5,6And Pharaoh said to Joseph, "Choose anywhere you like for them to live. Give them the best land of Egypt. The land of Goshen will be fine. And if any of them are capable, put them in charge of my flocks, too."

7Then Joseph brought his father Jacob to Pharaoh. And Jacob blessed Pharaoh.

8"How old are you?" Pharaoh asked him.

9Jacob replied, "I have lived 130 long, hard years, and I am not nearly as old as many of my ancestors." 10Then Jacob blessed Pharaoh again before he left.

11So Joseph assigned the best land of Egypt—the land of Rameses—to his father and brothers, just as Pharaoh had commanded. 12And Joseph furnished food to them in accordance with the number of their dependents.

The Famine Gets Worse

13The famine became worse and worse, so that all the land of Egypt and Canaan was starving. 14Joseph collected all the money in Egypt and Canaan in exchange for grain, and he brought the money to Pharaoh's treasure-houses. 15When the people were out of money, they came to Joseph crying again for food.

"Our money is gone," they said, "but give us bread; for why should we die?"

16"Well then," Joseph replied, "give me your livestock. I will trade you food in exchange."

17So they brought their cattle to Joseph in exchange for food. Soon all the horses, flocks, herds, and donkeys of Egypt were in Pharaoh's possession.

18The next year they came again and said, "Our money is gone, and our cattle are yours, and there is nothing left but our bodies and land. 19Why should we die? Buy us and our land and we will be serfs to Pharaoh. We will trade ourselves for food, then we will live, and the land won't be abandoned."

20So Joseph bought all the land of Egypt for Pharaoh; all the Egyptians sold him their fields because the famine was so severe. And the land became Pharaoh's. 21Thus all the people of Egypt became Pharaoh's serfs. 22The only land he didn't buy was that belonging to the priests, for they were assigned food from Pharaoh and didn't need to sell.

23Then Joseph said to the people, "See, I have bought you and your land for Pharaoh.

46:29 God approves of the outward expression of emotion. It is an honest display of feelings that draws us closer to others. To hide our feelings is a form of dishonesty. We need to learn to show our feelings in wise and loving ways. Our culture urges people to hide their feelings; we are expected to be stoic, even in times of extreme sorrow or joy. Jacob and Joseph embraced and wept a long while, openly displaying their emotions for all to see.

Here is grain. Go and sow the land. ²⁴And when you harvest it, a fifth of everything you get belongs to Pharaoh. Keep four parts for yourselves to be used for next year's seed, and as food for yourselves and for your households and little ones."

²⁵"You have saved our lives," they said. "We will gladly be the serfs of Pharaoh."

²⁶So Joseph made it a law throughout the land of Egypt—and it is still the law—that Pharaoh should have as his tax 20 percent of all the crops except those produced on the land owned by the temples.

Jacob Blesses Joseph's Sons
²⁷So Israel lived in the land of Goshen in Egypt, and soon the people of Israel began to prosper, and there was a veritable population explosion among them. ²⁸Jacob lived seventeen years after his arrival, so that he was 147 years old at the time of his death. ²⁹As the time drew near for him to die, he called for his son Joseph and said to him, "Swear to me most solemnly that you will honor this, my last request: do not bury me in Egypt. ³⁰But when I am dead, take me out of Egypt and bury me beside my ancestors." And Joseph promised. ³¹"Swear that you will do it," Jacob insisted. And Joseph did. Soon afterwards Jacob took to his bed.

CHAPTER 48
One day not long after this, word came to Joseph that his father was failing rapidly. So, taking with him his two sons, Manasseh and Ephraim, he went to visit him. ²When Jacob heard that Joseph had arrived, he gathered his strength and sat up in the bed to greet him, ³and said to him,

"God Almighty appeared to me at Luz in the land of Canaan and blessed me, ⁴and said to me, 'I will make you a great nation and I will give this land of Canaan to you and to your children's children, for an everlasting possession.' ⁵And now, as to these two sons of yours, Ephraim and Manasseh, born here in the land of Egypt before I arrived, I am adopting them as my own, and they will inherit from me just as Reuben and Simeon will. ⁶But

any other children born to you shall be your own, and shall inherit Ephraim's and Manasseh's portion from you. ⁷For your mother, Rachel, died after only two children when I came from Paddan-aram, as we were just a short distance from Ephrath, and I buried her beside the road to Bethlehem." ⁸Then Israel looked over at the two boys. "Are these the ones?" he asked.

⁹"Yes," Joseph told him, "these are my sons whom God has given me here in Egypt."

And Israel said, "Bring them over to me and I will bless them."

¹⁰Israel was half blind with age, so that he could hardly see. So Joseph brought the boys close to him and he kissed and embraced them.

¹¹And Israel said to Joseph, "I never thought that I would see you again, but now God has let me see your children too."

¹²,¹³Joseph took the boys by the hand, bowed deeply to him, and led the boys to their grandfather's knees—Ephraim at Israel's left hand and Manasseh at his right. ¹⁴But Israel crossed his arms as he stretched them out to lay his hands upon the boys' heads, so that his right hand was upon the head of Ephraim, the younger boy, and his left hand was upon the head of Manasseh, the older. He did this purposely.

¹⁵Then he blessed Joseph with this blessing: "May God, the God of my fathers Abraham and Isaac, the God who has shepherded me all my life, wonderfully bless these boys. ¹⁶He is the Angel who has kept me from all harm. May these boys be an honor to my name and to the names of my fathers Abraham and Isaac; and may they become a mighty nation."

¹⁷But Joseph was upset and displeased when he saw that his father had laid his right hand on Ephraim's head; so he lifted it to place it on Manasseh's head instead.

¹⁸"No, Father," he said. "You've got your right hand on the wrong head! This one over here is the older. Put your right hand on him!"

¹⁹But his father refused. "I know what I'm doing, my son," he said. "Manasseh too shall

48:1-9 Before blessing his grandsons, Ephraim and Manasseh, Jacob recalled the blessings that God had bestowed upon him. We know that the sins and failures of parents are often passed on to succeeding generations. But here we see that blessings are passed on as well. Abraham had established a relationship with God that he modeled before Isaac, which he then passed on to Jacob, and then to the succeeding generation. Let us establish the kind of relationship with God that will endure in the generations that follow. That way we will be able to bless our children with the blessings God has given us.

become a great nation, but his younger brother shall become even greater."

²⁰So Jacob blessed the boys that day with this blessing: "May the people of Israel bless each other by saying, 'God make you as prosperous as Ephraim and Manasseh.'" (Note that he put Ephraim before Manasseh.)

²¹Then Israel said to Joseph, "I am about to die, but God will be with you and will bring you again to Canaan, the land of your fathers. ²²And I have given the choice land of Shekem to you instead of to your brothers, as your portion of that land which I took from the Amorites with my sword and with my bow."

CHAPTER 49
Jacob Blesses His Sons
Then Jacob called together all his sons and said, "Gather around me and I will tell you what is going to happen to you in the days to come. ²Listen to me, O sons of Jacob; listen to Israel your father.

³"Reuben, you are my oldest son, the child of my vigorous youth. You are the head of the list in rank and in honor. ⁴But you are unruly as the wild waves of the sea, and you shall be first no longer. I am demoting you, for you slept with one of my wives and thus dishonored me.

⁵"Simeon and Levi are two of a kind. They are men of violence and injustice. ⁶O my soul, stay away from them. May I never be a party to their wicked plans. For in their anger they murdered a man, and maimed oxen just for fun. ⁷Cursed be their anger, for it is fierce and cruel. Therefore, I will scatter their descendants throughout Israel.

⁸"Judah, your brothers shall praise you. You shall destroy your enemies. Your father's sons shall bow before you. ⁹Judah is a young lion that has finished eating its prey. He has settled down as a lion—who will dare to rouse him? ¹⁰The scepter shall not depart from Judah until Shiloh comes, whom all people shall obey. ¹¹He has chained his steed to the choicest vine

and washed his clothes in wine. ¹²His eyes are darker than wine and his teeth are whiter than milk.

¹³"Zebulun shall dwell on the shores of the sea and shall be a harbor for ships, with his borders extending to Sidon.

¹⁴"Issachar is a strong beast of burden resting among the saddlebags. ¹⁵When he saw how good the countryside was, how pleasant the land, he willingly bent his shoulder to the task and served his masters with vigor.

¹⁶"Dan shall govern his people like any other tribe in Israel. ¹⁷He shall be a serpent in the path that bites the horses' heels, so that the rider falls off. ¹⁸I trust in your salvation, Lord.

¹⁹"A marauding band shall stamp upon Gad, but he shall rob and pursue them!

²⁰"Asher shall produce rich foods, fit for kings!

²¹"Naphtali is a deer let loose, producing lovely fawns.

²²"Joseph is a fruitful tree beside a fountain. His branches shade the wall. ²³He has been severely injured by those who shot at him and persecuted him, ²⁴but their weapons were shattered by the Mighty One of Jacob, the Shepherd, the Rock of Israel. ²⁵May the God of your fathers, the Almighty, bless you with blessings of heaven above and of the earth beneath—blessings of the breasts and of the womb, ²⁶blessings of the grain and flowers, blessings reaching to the utmost bounds of the everlasting hills. These shall be the blessings upon the head of Joseph who was exiled from his brothers.

²⁷"Benjamin is a wolf that prowls. He devours his enemies in the morning, and in the evening divides the loot."

²⁸So these are the blessings that Israel, their father, blessed his twelve sons with.

Jacob Dies and Is Buried
²⁹,³⁰Then he told them, "Soon I will die. You must bury me with my fathers in the land of

---

49:5-7 Simeon and Levi were characterized by violent tempers, and the history of these brothers in Genesis corroborates Jacob's assessment. After their sister Dinah was raped, they took revenge by deceiving and slaughtering all the men of the city (34:1-31). This tendency needed to be curbed. Many years later, however, when God called out for people to stand on his side, the Levites stood forth and vigorously defended God's cause (see Exodus 32:25-29). As a result, they were chosen as God's priests in Israel. Let us look to God to transform our weaknesses into strengths, just as he did with the descendants of Levi.

49:13-27 The remarks by Jacob concerning each of his sons seem very harsh, but the information he shared, including a confession of his own failure as a father, should have given helpful direction to each of them. We have a lot to learn from our parents, but often they aren't willing to be honest with us. Or if they are, we aren't really ready to listen. We need to learn both to speak honestly and to listen with respect.

Canaan, in the cave in the field of Mach-pelah, facing Mamre—the field Abraham bought from Ephron the Hethite for a burial ground. ³¹There they buried Abraham and Sarah, his wife; there they buried Isaac and Rebekah, his wife; and there I buried Leah. ³²It is the cave which my grandfather Abraham purchased from the sons of Heth." ³³Then, when Jacob had finished his prophecies to his sons, he lay back in the bed, breathed his last, and died.

CHAPTER 50
Joseph threw himself upon his father's body and wept over him and kissed him. ²Afterwards he commanded his morticians to embalm the body. ³The embalming process required forty days, with a period of national mourning of seventy days. ⁴Then, when at last the mourning was over, Joseph approached Pharaoh's staff and requested them to speak to Pharaoh on his behalf.

⁵"Tell His Majesty," he requested them, "that Joseph's father made Joseph swear to take his body back to the land of Canaan, to bury him there. Ask His Majesty to permit me to go and bury my father; assure him that I will return promptly."

⁶Pharaoh agreed. "Go and bury your father, as you promised," he said.

⁷So Joseph went, and a great number of Pharaoh's counselors and assistants—all the senior officers of the land, ⁸as well as all of Joseph's people—his brothers and their families. But they left their little children and flocks and herds in the land of Goshen. ⁹So a very great number of chariots, cavalry, and people accompanied Joseph.

¹⁰When they arrived at Atad (meaning "Threshing Place of Brambles"), beyond the Jordan River, they held a very great and solemn funeral service, with a seven-day period of lamentation for Joseph's father. ¹¹The local residents, the Canaanites, renamed the place Abel-mizraim (meaning "Egyptian Mourners") for they said, "It is a place of very deep mourning by these Egyptians." ¹²,¹³So his sons did as Israel commanded them, and carried his body into the land of Canaan and buried it there in the cave of Mach-pelah—the cave Abraham had bought in the field of Ephron the Hethite, close to Mamre.

¹⁴Then Joseph returned to Egypt with his brothers and all who had accompanied him to the funeral of his father.

Joseph Reassures His Brothers
¹⁵But now that their father was dead, Joseph's brothers were frightened.

"Now Joseph will pay us back for all the evil we did to him," they said. ¹⁶,¹⁷So they sent him this message: "Before he died, your father instructed us to tell you to forgive us for the great evil we did to you. We servants of the God of your father beg you to forgive us." When Joseph read the message, he broke down and cried.

¹⁸Then his brothers came and fell down before him and said, "We are your slaves."

¹⁹But Joseph told them, "Don't be afraid of me. Am I God, to judge and punish you? ²⁰As far as I am concerned, God turned into good what you meant for evil, for he brought me to this high position I have today so that I could save the lives of many people. ²¹No, don't be afraid. Indeed, I myself will take care of you and your families." And he spoke very kindly to them, reassuring them.

²²So Joseph and his brothers and their families continued to live in Egypt. Joseph was 110 years old when he died. ²³He lived to see the birth of his son Ephraim's children, and the children of Machir, Manasseh's son, who played at his feet.

²⁴"Soon I will die," Joseph told his brothers, "but God will surely come and get you, and bring you out of this land of Egypt and take you back to the land he promised to the descendants of Abraham, Isaac and Jacob." ²⁵Then Joseph made his brothers promise with an oath that they would take his body back with them when they returned to Canaan. ²⁶So Joseph died at the age of 110, and they embalmed him, and his body was placed in a coffin in Egypt.

50:15-21 When Jacob died, Joseph's brothers feared that he would take revenge for their past differences. They thought Joseph had spared them only for the sake of their father. Here they discovered that Joseph's forgiveness was complete, with no ulterior motives. Joseph had already granted his brothers complete forgiveness; his brothers couldn't believe it and thus had not yet received it. They had needlessly lived in fear of a coming punishment. God hands us forgiveness that is just as complete, but we need to believe it, and then receive it. Only then can we experience the freedom he offers.

REFLECTIONS ON
GENESIS

❋insights FROM THE NAMES OF GOD

The Hebrew name for God used in **Genesis 1:1** (*Elohim*) demonstrates the enormity of God's power to transform lives. This name for God is in the plural form, signifying his strength and might. It also hints that God is in some sense plural—a community unto himself (see also 1:26; 3:22; 11:7). But though this name is plural, it is treated grammatically as singular, revealing God's unified and personal nature. He is omnipotent in power, but personal in his touch. He is able and willing to provide the help we need.

In **Genesis 2:4** a new Hebrew name for God is introduced: "Lord" (*Yahweh* or *Jehovah*). This is the personal name for God; it is his relationship name. It describes the God who chose Abraham and established a covenant with him. It describes the God who chose to relate to the Israelites and make them his people. It is the name that reminds us that God wants to have a relationship with us.

❋insights FROM GOD'S CREATION

As the source of all things, God is always able to meet our needs. The Hebrew verb translated "create" in **Genesis 1:1** describes an act that only God can do; and it is used to describe three things that science cannot explain: the creation of something from nothing (1:1), the creation of living things from inanimate matter (1:21-22), and the creation of man (1:27). A God who can create people and the world we live in can certainly empower a person in the process of recovery.

Genesis 1:2 describes the earth before it was shaped by God's creative hand. It was shapeless, chaotic, and dark. These three characteristics forebode nothing but trouble. But then we are told that "the Spirit of God [was] brooding over the dark vapors." This fourth characteristic is a source of hope and promises recovery. The presence of the Holy Spirit was a necessary element in the events of all six days of creation. In the same way, his presence in our life is necessary before any rebuilding and recovery can take place.

In **Genesis 1:3** God said, "Let there be light." The word *Let* in this verse is used to introduce one of God's purposes for his creation—that there should be light in the world. This word is used repeatedly in this chapter to introduce the various things that God intended for his creation (see 1:6, 9, 11, 14-15, 20, 24, 26). He had a purpose and plan for everything. He also has a plan for each of us. And his plan is designed to bring about the best for his creation. We need only be willing to turn our recovery over to his design and plan.

In **Genesis 1:26-27** we see that the first people were created to be like God. Oceans of ink have been spilled attempting to explain what this means. One characteristic that all the writers agree upon is the ability of people to make moral decisions. We have the power of choice, and we are accountable to God and to others for the choices we make. To continue in recovery we must take responsibility for this aspect of God's nature that is alive and well in each of us.

❋insights ABOUT TEMPTATION

In **Genesis 2:16-17** God forbade Adam and Eve to eat from a single tree. Why did he do this? Why didn't God create a world where people couldn't sin? Or why didn't he make people so they couldn't disobey his commands? The answer lies in the very nature of God. God is love and desires to have a loving relationship with his creatures. He wants us to respond to him with love in return. But a loving response is only possible when we have the choice to do otherwise. He wants us to obey because we love him, not because we have no other choice.

In **Genesis 1:1-3** Satan began his temptation of Eve by planting doubt in her mind concerning what God had said. Notice that Eve wasn't very clear on the details of God's command. God had told them not to *eat* fruit from a certain tree (2:17). Eve claimed that God had said they were not even to *touch* the tree. She was making God's requirements more difficult than God himself had done! Her own confusion about what God had said made her even more susceptible to the serpent's wiles. We will need a proper understanding of God's truth if we hope to stand against Satan's temptations.

In **Genesis 3:6** notice that Eve quickly succumbed to a visual temptation. Until Eve really *saw* the tree, she was not influenced by the three common elements of all temptation. She saw that the tree was good for food ("the lust of the flesh"), it looked lovely and fresh ("the lust of the eyes"), and it was a tree that would make her wise ("the pride of life"). These are still important weapons in Satan's arsenal of temptation (see 1 John 2:16).

✳*insights* ABOUT SIN AND ITS CONSEQUENCES

In **Genesis 3:7** Adam and Eve became aware of their nakedness. With their act of disobedience came embarrassment and shame. They did their best to cover themselves; they didn't like what they saw when they looked at themselves. This happens to all of us when we sin and when we become dependent on cruel addictions. We don't like what we see, so we cover it up with lies and half-truths. And we do it to preserve our relationships. But in the end, our intimacy with others is destroyed. We need to be honest with ourselves and others and work at reestablishing our relationships. This is a significant part of our recovery.

In **Genesis 3:10** Adam admitted that he was hiding from God. One of the terrible consequences of our sin is the isolation that results. We want to hide from other people; we want to hide from God. Our failures will always make us want to hide. But recovery means that we must bring our sin out into the open; this will then bring us back into our relationships—with others and with God.

In **Genesis 3:15** it becomes obvious that Adam and Eve are powerless in the face of the sin question. Alone, they cannot overwhelm Satan and escape the temptations he offers. In his grace, God promised that the offspring of the woman would defeat Satan. He promised that he would take charge of the recovery process and overcome the enemy. This is good news—the first mention of the gospel of grace that would eventually be fulfilled by the coming of Jesus, the Messiah.

In **Genesis 3:18-19** we see that after the Fall, even the earth responded differently to its human masters. In the beginning it was their constant ally, yielding its fruits easily to their hands. But now, it brought forth thorns and thistles and weeds. Work became an arduous task, frustrating and unfulfilling.

There was no reason for Adam and Eve to expect to live on after their failure. God had clearly stated that the consequences of their sin would be death (see 2:17). Yet in **Genesis 3:20** Adam displayed his faith in our gracious God by naming his wife Eve, which means "the life-giving one." He believed that she would live to be the mother of the human race. Adam's faith in God gave him hope for the future, even when his past gave him little to hope for.

✳*insights* FROM CAIN AND ABEL

In **Genesis 4:4** Abel slew an innocent substitute as his offering, and God accepted him. Abel was obedient to God's instructions. Our relationship with God can be established by accepting God's gracious forgiveness and allowing the innocent sacrifice of his Son to stand in our place. Abel's sacrifice of one of his lambs was the second death mentioned in the Bible.

In **Genesis 4:5** we see that God rejected Cain's offering. We may wonder why this was so. We don't have all the details, but we do know that his offering was given in rebellion (see Jude 1:11). Apparently Cain wanted to do things his way; he didn't want to follow the program that God had mapped out for this first human family. Notice that Cain responded first with disappointment. He wanted to be accepted by God, but he wanted to earn divine approval by his hard work in the fields. God could not accept his gift of farm produce. Acceptance by God cannot be bought with hard work; we need to admit our need and humbly allow a sacrifice to stand in our place. God has provided us with the perfect sacrifice in the person of Jesus Christ. He stands in our place, paying for all our failures and sins, freeing us to start again.

✳*insights* FROM NOAH'S LIFE

After years of waiting, God saw that the human race still refused to live according to his plan. In **Genesis 6:5-6** we see that things were getting worse, not better. This broke God's heart because of the great love he had for his creation. It should encourage us to know that God doesn't punish us in anger. He does it for our good because he loves us.

In **Genesis 6:7** God promises to judge his fallen and sinful creation. Even though God is patient with us and gives us many chances to change our ways, we cannot act with impunity. Because he is righteous, God must act to protect innocent people who are hurt by sin.

God had assigned Noah the monumental task of rebuilding human society on earth. But God didn't just hand Noah the task and walk away. In **Genesis 9:9-13** God promises to support Noah's work and sets a rainbow in the sky as a seal of his promise. Many of us are rebuilding, too. We can be sure that God will support our recovery with his presence and promises. And we should keep an eye out for the "rainbows" along the way. God often leaves us signs to remind us of his loving presence and care.

insights FROM ABRAHAM'S LIFE

In **Genesis 12:2-3** God gave Abram some special promises. He would make Abram a great nation; he would bless him and make him famous; and he would make Abram a blessing to others. God promised to bless those who blessed Abram and to curse those who cursed him. Notice that God's promises to Abram illustrate Step Twelve in recovery. After receiving God's blessing, Abram was to turn around and share it with others.

Initially Abram responded with half-obedience to God's call, moving with his family from Ur to Haran (11:31-32). **Genesis 12:4,** however, indicates the beginning of Abram's radical obedience to God. Having discovered God's will, Abram became willing to do what God's plan required of him. Our recovery begins when we learn to seek God's will and become willing to follow it without reservation.

We may wonder what Abram expected the Promised Land to be like. In **Genesis 12:10** we see that he arrived to find the land ravaged by famine. It probably wasn't what he had expected or hoped for, but it was the place that God had intended for him and his descendants. There will be times in recovery when things are difficult. Sometimes we may need to do things that we are not comfortable doing. But we need to follow God—even when his program doesn't lead us down the paths we had expected or hoped for.

The lie that Abram told in **Genesis 12:11-13** showed that he lacked faith in God. He didn't believe that God would protect him, so he took things into his own hands. We may feel that a little lie is justified if it is intended to protect something important to us. We may even succeed in getting away with it for a while, but all lies reap long-term consequences. It is best to trust God to protect us as we tell the truth. The God of truth will stand with us as we step out in faith.

In **Genesis 22:8-13** we find Abraham about to sacrifice his son Isaac. Much to the relief of Abraham and Isaac, however, God provided a substitute. We do not know what Abraham had in mind when he told his son that God would provide a sacrifice, but we do know that God has provided a sacrifice for us—not simply a ram caught in a thicket, but his only Son. Anyone who believes in him will have the means for discovering a new life now, and through eternity as well.

insights FROM JOSEPH'S LIFE

Many commentators have noted that nothing bad is ever said about Joseph. That may be true of his adult life, but as a boy he was irritatingly overconfident. In **Genesis 37:2** we see that he was also a tattletale. Joseph's arrogant behavior as a youth, along with his father's favoritism, planted seeds of hatred in his brothers' hearts. Joseph consequently suffered years of slavery in Egypt. Joseph was certainly more worthy of praise than his brothers, but he can hardly be given perfect marks.

In **Genesis 39:19-23** we see that God was with Joseph even in prison. We are told that he prospered in everything he did. And through all his trials, Joseph remained faithful to God. It would have been easy for him to start playing the victim and just give up. When we play the victim, we start to blame others and lose our ability to act. We need to stop blaming and start acting, doing our best in the situations in which God places us.

In **Genesis 50:15-21** a clear message comes across: man proposes but God disposes. Joseph's brothers intended their actions toward Joseph for evil, but God turned those actions into good. It is wonderful that God can veto our foolish plans, transforming our mistakes and failures into the means for his gracious purposes.